VIEW FROM T

Tommy lives with his grandparents in the backstreets of Gateshead on the Tyne. His grandmother, Bella, watches over her rather wayward family with a stern but kindly eye. She particularly has to keep a watch over her husband, Nobbler, who has an unfortunate way of making hard-earned money vanish.

From his perch on the fender, little Tommy watches the antics of the grown-ups and forms his own vision of the future - a future which is to include an apprenticeship at the local foundry, and entry into the R.A.F. just before the outbreak of World War II.

"I read *View from the Fender* with great enjoyment. Right from the beginning the characters walked off the page: their conversation, their actions and reactions, were so true to life." Catherine Cookson

VIEW FROM THE FENDER

by

Tom Shaughnessy

ROBERT HALE · LONDON

First published in Great Britain 1987

First paperback edition 1990

ISBN 0 7090 3838 0

Robert Hale Limited
Clerkenwell House
Clerkenwell Green
London EC1R 0HT

Printed in Great Britain by WBC Print Ltd, Barton Manor, Bristol.

Contents

Part Six

Part Seven

Part Eight

PART ONE

Nobbler

Nobbler Dobson gazed in dismay at the back page of the Evening Chronicle.

'The bugger's gone doon!' he snorted. He shifted his gaze across to Bella, his wife. She wasn't impressed. Why should she be, she'd heard it all before.

She contemplated Tom, half-hidden in the shadow cast by the light of the back window of their lower flat, the light from the window illuminating Tom's bad news. She wasn't interested whether 'it' had gone up or doon. There were other things to contemplate; for instance her good fortune at moving across from the other side of the street. This flat was not only sixpence a week cheaper, the information about the new flush lavatories had been correct. It was true that the even numbers were converted first. Much superior to those dry middens.

She'd moved downstairs to save her legs. It was difficult to run a shop upstairs. That was another good move. The coal business was still in the upstairs-flat backyard. She was, she mused, not doing badly. Tom, 'Nobbler', he wasn't happy.

'It's gone doon!' It was a statement that called for sympathy. He got none. Not from Bella.

She sniffed. 'Daft buzzer, Tom! Sarves you right. You and yor horses. Bettin' is for mugs. Waste of good money, that's what it is.' She slipped her hands into her money pockets. It was an automatic gesture. These were special pockets made of strong striped material. They were not unlike soldiers' ammunition pouches; one hung each side of her like a man's trouser pockets. The coins inside rattled as she gripped them firmly.

Tom knew that move, it meant, 'That's yor lot for this week!'

'Ah thought it was a sure thing. It was the form horse.' Tom shook his head, bewildered. 'The system mustn't be workin'.'

'System? System?' Bella snorted and her coinage rattled. 'Be more use if you got out with the gallawa on yor roond.'

Nobbler didn't want to think about his horse and cart and that coal-round. That Bella, she just didn't understand.

As for Bella, she had her little shop and local money-lending scheme. She wasn't really a money-lender, just doing folk a favour at two-and-six in the pound. If you didn't have ready money for flour or tea or sugar or soap, or any other of the limited items she sold, you could borrow a few shillins'. Those money bags, handy at her sides and underneath her apron, carried many shillins' and half-crowns; even a few ten-bob notes too. Bella was nothing if not entirely practical. She had to be with such a dreamer for a husband. At least one of her four sons could be the same. Her three daughters, well, daughters, they weren't as useless as men, at least they could clean the house.

The neighbours regarded Bella as tight-fisted, especially those who borrowed. Those on the Gardians had a top rate of five bob; most were. Only those with a job could borrow ten bob. Nobody in the Teams district was rich enough to borrow a quid.

'Better to be the bookie than the backer.'

Bella's words brought life back to Tom. 'Eh?'

Tom's immediate reaction caused those hands to grip the

financial department tighter than ever. Bella knew she'd said too much. Perhaps her mate would miss the point. He didn't.

'Got to have a stake to be a bookie!' Tom looked across to Bella, now hunched in a defensive square-shaped bundle of four petticoats and two aprons. Was she really interested? She was, but only in protecting her wealth.

'Why do you need a stake?' she asked.

Tom was thrown by that. What was the lass talking about. Still, that was women for you, they just didn't understand.

'Why does a bookie need a stake?' He was asking himself as well as Bella.

'Aye, why do you need a stake? Whoever heered of a bookie losin'.'

'Er,' Tom almost snorted. 'Every bugger knows a bookie needs a pot to start with. He might have to pay out.'

'Pay out? Why yor daft lad. Bookies canna lose! How can they? They mek all the rules and hold the stake money ... So how can they lose?'

How can bookies lose? A bewildering question. Women just didn't understand. Tom sighed, all that women thought about was washin' and cleanin' and hanging curtains. They just didn't understand. Why, he knew how much Stan Black took in every Saturday; Stan took in almost thirty quid. Thirty quid? Tom shuddered at the thought, and most of that at ten to one. Three hundred quid to pay out if everybody won.

'Do you know how much Stan Black would have to pay out on Saturday if everybody backed a winner?' Tom showed his superiority to Bella. She spent too much time countin' pennies. She didn't know that Tom, as Stan Black's chief runner, was in a position to know all about this heady finance.

Bella shook her head. No, she didn't know how much Stan Black would have to pay out if everybody backed a winner. She knew at least one mug who wouldn't win.

'Three hundred quid!' Tom announced it as if it was a

State secret. 'Mind you, Bella, you keep that to yorsel!' His eyes fell on to the little fellow sitting on the fender. 'Take yor thumb out of your mouth, son.' He smiled at his grandson, little Tommy. 'Little tinker is takin' it all in.'

Little Tommy's eyes had flicked back and forth from Granda to Grandma. He took his thumb out of his mouth obediently. It was back in again when the conversation continued on the local high finance.

The fender as a seat was the warmest in the house. You could, if you were the right size and disposition, slide back and forth, the fender being polished to a mirror finish. Behind Tommy's back was the oven. He wasn't permitted to sit in front of the glowing fire. First for safety reasons, because coal fires sometimes contain stones which burst and spit, and 'You make a better door than a winder, lad, let's see the fire.'

The fire was the chief focal point. It consumed coal, and Bella sold coal, she was never without a healthy glowing hearth. The iron fireplace-range, equipped with the oven on the left, was balanced with the hot-water tank opposite. The fire filled the middle ground, heating both the oven and the water tank. A dog-plate controlled the temperature of the oven, from which glorious smells emanated twice a week.

Friday was the day for, 'gettin' the thick off!' It was the day when everything in and around the fireplace was hauled out and polished. Baking of teacake and brown and white bread took place after that weekly overhaul. The fire was banked up at night and cow-heel and stewing-steak roasted quietly in preparation for the week-end. The fender had a further bright sparkle and the three it guarded had a sombre brightness from black-lead polish.

The fender controlled the ashes which fell from the high-level coal fire. The fire also served as a waste disposal unit. That fire could consume almost anything and it was served by a chimney big enough to allow entry to Father Christmas. Even at that thumb-sucking age, our little observer on the fender pondered how the toy-carrier could get down that soot-covered chimney without setting fire to his beard.

In well-run houses the ashes were carried outside every day without fail. Bella's was a well-run house. If she didn't do all the work herself, she could organize others to do it. Of her three daughters, 'Our Annie', the little observer's mother, was the 'major-domo'. Nobody but 'our Annie' was allowed to touch coal, flour, or money and the wafer-thin Sunday tea-set. A tea-set you could see through when it was held to the light, so 'femma' (fragile) that boiling water had to be, according to Bella's instruction, 'well off the boil, our Annie', when the tea-set was washed.

As well as serving as the observer's seat, the fender was a step up to the head-level mantelpiece, a shelf for whatever a particular household wished to display. Most in that poor part of Gateshead had nothing. Bella's display would not shame the Lady of the Manor.

Bella's brass candlesticks were the envy of all who called at Bella's, and especially Miss Mulligan, the ticket woman, 'a lady altogether'. Miss Mulligan must have been a lady, she wore a hat ... everyday!

Bella never wore a 'lady's hat' except for christenings, weddings and funerals, or those few visits she had to the seaside. On cold days she wore one of Tom's caps, the gaffer's cap.

If Bella lived in the poorer part of Gateshead, she wasn't poor of business instinct. Her house was local centre for distribution of tickets and a clearing centre for local gossip. If Bella didn't know about it, it hadn't happened.

Was Bella getting a 'rake-off' from Miss Mulligan? Miss Mulligan held her china cup with her little finger held high, how could anybody think such thoughts? 'If she doesn't get a thrupenny-bit for each ticket, she'll still get her tiddly!' the know-it-alls would nod. They didn't mind that, if it was true. What they didn't like were Tom's pigeons. Tom kept hens and pigeons. Hens now, they could be a good investment, but pigeons, ugh! They were messy buggers! Bella said so many times. Nobbler wouldn't budge. When it came to the crunch – and it never did – Nobbler was the boss! In mitigation he could always point to Bella's pride and joy, the hand-painted china tea-set and say, 'There-yar, Bella, they's got pigeons and pigeon crees in China.' He would point out the oriental gentleman doing a balancing act with two birds on a pole, facing a pagoda. He would turn to the little observer on the fender and say, holding up a cup, 'Who's that, Tombo?' Tombo would reply obediently, 'That's Granda and Blackie and Whitey and Granda's cree.' That's what Nobbler's interpretation of his grandson's garble was.

Nobbler the Bookie

'He's a clivver lad, little Tombo!' Nobbler winked at Bella. 'Recognized his Granda right away. That's me playin' quoits, on the other side.' He turned the china cup around.

'Bah, you and yor quoits and yor pigeons and yor bettin'. Wouldn't be so bad if you could pick a few winners.'

'Ah'm Teams champion!' Nobbler blurted. 'Best quoit player in the district!' That should impress her. It didn't.

'And how much does that bring in?' she snapped.

'Bring in? Nowt, ah suppose. But it's good bein' champion!' Nobbler beamed at the little thumb-sucker on the fender. 'See, the littlin' knows how to get ringers.'

Bella snorted. 'Champion quoit player? More use to me if you get that gallawa out and be the champion coal-seller! You, you little tinker, get yor thumb out of yor mouth! Here's a hapenny, go to Hanna's and get yorsel a taffy-cake.'

The thumb came out of that mouth like magic at the sound of that name, Hanna's. Hanna had a small sweet-shop in her parlour. If you were little, she would help you up on to the long form that ran the length of the sweets on display. There you could sit almost endlessly, wondering what you could do without. It could be harrowing when you had only one hapenny.

Hanna's taffee cakes were famous. You could break one into three or four bits and they could last all afternoon. Should your tongue happen upon the paper mould while sampling the sweetness, well, sweet paper was just as sweet as taffee. It was when the supply in your pockets got stuck in the threads of your trousers; that was crisis-time.

Tombo knew the drill. The thumb in the mouth always opened the cash box. He was bribed every day and every day he succeeded in his ploy. When would they twig? But you couldn't put your thumb in your mouth alongside Hanna's taffee cake. That was impossible!

Bella had eight children. Five sons and three daughters. Thomas, the eldest son, had been killed in the Great War. With that tragedy still dogging her she got on with the task of organizing the rest, plus her dreamer of a husband.

'The youngin' could get six hapennies from the Sheenys for lightin' their gas on Friday.' Nobbler grinned as the littlin' scooted off to Hanna's.

'That's our Lizzie's job! I'll not have him skivvyin' for any Sheeny. Anyway, aal Jews is not Sheenys! That Annie Summerfield, she's a real lady, and all the way from Russia. Aye, and her man, Yenkill Summerfield, he's a real gent; calls our Annie Mrs. Billie so he'll know the difference.'

'Aah thought that aal Jews come from Jewland? How come Annie Summerfield comes from Russia?' Nobbler reflected.

'How do aah know! Aal ah know is that she's too good for the bugger she's married to! Like aal women.'

Nobbler grinned. If he was put down by that he tried not to show it. He knew that Bella was firm rather than hard. He changed the direction.

'Pity you couldn't get a, what's it called, er, mona, er, first chance, to do for the Jews every Friday?' He knew how to feed Bella's commercial interest.

Bella missed Nobbler's twinkle because of the gleam in her eye. Yes, it would be a good idea if she could get a monopoly on doin' for the Jews every Friday.

'Crafty buggers, the Jews,' Nobbler observed. 'Our Annie found a ten-bob note under the settee at Jacksons. They put it there to see if she moved the furniture instead of just cleanin' around.'

'Aye, the Jews know what it's aal about. They believe in value for money.' Bella nodded in sympathetic agreement. 'Our Annie is too soft, but aal Jews is not stingy. Them Summerfields is different to them Cowans.'

'Cohens you mean! He's a solicitor, isn't he?'

'Cohens, Cowans, what does it matter? How do you make that out, Tom?'

'Well, if he aint a solicitor, the bugger must be one of Lauderdale's men. Them and solicitors dress the same. Same black suit and lang face.' Nobbler chuckled at those sombre faces.

'Aye, they's never out of business. Undertakers and solicitors always had money comin' in.'

'Aye, nee risk there. Them fellas has their first penny.'

'We can't say the same about you, can we?' Bella sniffed.

'Aye, lass, but yor good enough for both of us! Yor both undertaker and solicitor for the district, and you does it for nowt!'

For nowt? Bella paled at the thought. But she did. She did for the district. The other matriarchs made her the chief and it was her house that held the winding-laying-out sheets. A knock in the night still startled her. It would he Tom that went to the door and then came back to bed to say, 'It's for you, lass. They want you.'

She would go to the door and the whisper through the door from without would say, 'Can we have the sheets, Bella? Can you give us a hand?' Somebody needed laying out, ready for Lauderdale. Bella, as chief matriarch, would join the others.

Should there be any argument about the division of goods and chattels stemming from that death, it would be Bella who would be called upon to adjudicate.

Her good advice had a sting in its tail. God help you if you didn't wear black for a month. God help you if you took down your fanlight shade and drew your window shades before the appointed time. If you were a woman, God help you if you looked at another man within two years. God might help you, Bella would cut you dead!

'You was sayin', about, havin' nee pot to start a book?' Nobbler approached the delicate matter cautiously.

Yes, it was a most delicate matter and Bella showed it by grasping right and left money pouches even more firmly. While her hand was in, no other hand could enter. She had entered risky territory. She knew now that she should have let Tom go on losing a few shillings each week. Perhaps that would be the cheapest way of controlling his craving?

'Ah never lend ten bob unless there's a Sunday suit in the family.' Her lips tightened and the pert nose lifted two inches. 'Don't you get too near to that fire, you little tinker.' The little tinker moved obediently back to his station in front of the oven.

Nobbler stood in front of the fire, as was his right. With thumbs in his waist-coat he thought it out.

'Ah's got a Sunday suit, but it'll still take more than ten bob to start a book, lass!' He wasn't begging, just testing the water. He turned to the fire and washed his hands in the reflected heat. He winked to the upturned face, from the fender.

'Her upstairs, Cilla (another matriarch), she makes them leave their clock before she lends a pund!'

Nobbler turned from the fire and resumed his position with thumbs in waistcoat. He gazed enquiringly at his mate.

'Oh aye, she would, wouldn't she!' He didn't quite see the point. Cilla was a rival, she wanted to sell coal too.

He finally gave in. 'What's ma Sunday suit and other folks' clocks got to do with startin' a book?'

'It's what the nobs call, col-at-eral.' Bella was hesitant about that important word.

'Col-at-eral?'

'Aye, Miss Mulligan told me. It's like money in the bank, but it's not money.' Bella's explanation shed no light to Tom. Ten bob or ten pund in his hand, he understood that. Light did dawn at last. He now knew, or thought he knew, what Bella meant.

'Like when our Jane pops Big Dan's suit every Monday?'

'Aye lad, aye! If that big bugger gave the lass more money and stayed off the beer, she wouldn't have to pop his suit. Mind you, Tom, you stay out of it. Never interfere!'

Nobbler frowned. He didn't like Big Dan, his son-in-law. He was meaning to have words with him about his behaviour. Aye, the lass was right. Some women were married to the wrong men.

Bella's right hand came out of her pocket. She poked a finger at Nobbler. 'Mind, you stay out of it. Never interfere between man and wife. As long as there's no bairns, let them fight it out between their-sels!' The pointed finger was accompanied with a knowing nod toward the littlin'. Grown-ups didn't discuss marital matters in the presence of youngins'.

Nobbler said, 'Aye.' It was a growl rather than an acknowledgement. His thumbs came out of his waistcoat and his fists clenched. Bella knew the signs. Those fists could go flying at somebody. She used some balm to calm

Nobbler.

'Bookies is outside the law! Bookies doesn't need col-at-eral! Back-lane bookies, ah mean.'

'Ah know that! That's why that bugger Corrigan is always chasin' me. Coppers is too big to catch the lads.' Nobbler grinned as he thought of the lumbering policeman. He could take refuge in any of the scores of houses in the district should Corrigan spot him taking bets for Stan Black. Aye, for Stan Black, taking money for Stan Black, and he, Nobbler, with other runners, was makin' money for bookies. Bella was right, he was a mug, takin' money to Stan Black when he could keep that money for his-sel.

'Why is back-lane bookin' agin the law, lass? The nobs can gamble when they're racin'. The king goes racin'. He has a few bob on, I'll be bound.' He tried to imagine the king being chased by Corrigan. 'Aye, a law for the rich and a different law for the lads,' he grumbled.

'The nobs who make the law know what they's doin'. Folks like you have to be minded against their-sels. Don't you know you canna win? If bookies could lose, there wouldn't be any! But you canna blame the bookies, there's always plenty of mugs around ready and willin' to give away their hard-earned.' Bella was exasperated. Why couldn't Tom see. He was beginning to.

'So, bookies doesn't need a pot? They doesn't need this, er, col-at-eral? It's a bit risky though, hinny? Ah'd need bloody lang legs if everybody won! Supposin' a fella got a tip that came in at twenty to one and they had two pund on? Ky-Wy had a twenty to one last week and Stan had to pay out.' It wasn't all as easy as Bella had said. Nobbler had that uneasy feeling.

Bella snorted like an angry buffalo. She shifted her seat and her chair grazed against her precious polished press. That made her mad.

'Silly bugger! Ky-Wy tips every horse in a race. He's bound to give that horse to some mug seein' he sells a different tip in every back-lane.' Her voice had risen to a shriek.

Nobbler backed off in alarm. Was that how Ky-Wy was a good tipper? Did he really tip every horse in the race? The honest, gullible Nobbler never thought crafty thoughts. But he was learnin'. He resumed his gaffer's stance at the fire-place and with thumbs in his waistcoat pockets announced, 'How do you pay out a twenty to one with two pund on without a pot?' That would put Bella down. She'd have no answer to that. But she had!

Bella, after having eight children and in at the birth of dozens of others, wasn't likely to be put down so easily.

'Why you silly lad.' It was as if she was talking to a bairn. 'All you do is pass it on! If you has a risky bet, you just lay it off. Haven't you learned owt from Stan? Miss Mulligan calls it sharing the risk. Aah told you, bookies canna lose!' Bella nodded benignly at her mate.

Nobbler was the gaffer. He knew about women, all they knew about was washin' bairns and wallpaper and donkey-stonin' the scullery and the front step. He looked at Bella like a wise man looks at a novice.

'How'ma gonna make a bit if ah lays it all off?' Those sharp blue eyes looked askance at Bella. The thumbs dug deeper into the gaffer's waistcoat.

Bella's mild attitude disappeared. She scowled back at Nobbler. She had ceased to be a dreamer years ago. The facts of a hard life had taught her a little profit every week if not every day was a better proposition than Nobbler's daily dream of a big treble win. Men, they was just grown-up bairns!

'Trouble with you, Tom, you want to get rich too soon! You doesn't lay it all off, just the big bets. You rely on the thrupenny bets for a bit of good!' Bella settled back in her chair simmering. She hunched her money pockets on to her knees as if they'd be safer there.

Nobbler said, 'Oh aye!' It was obvious he didn't think

much of the profit from thrupenny bets. He turned to the fire and gave his hands a good dry wash. The flaming coals got his attention as if they could solve his problem.

'Ah could make more money sellin' squibs for Father Cassidy,' he told the fire, or Bella, if she was in the mood to listen.

Bella snorted at that. Those high-laced boots beat a quick tattoo on the little mat that was part of her personal corner between the press, the square table and 'her' carved sideboard behind. What treasures she had, were well at hand. You'd have to shift her first to get at them. Only 'Our Annie' the major-domo, had access to that corner.

'Yor not a Catholic and Father Cassidy will still expect you to sell squibs for nowt, just like aal good Catholics!' She'd taken her hands out of her pockets and now sat with arms folded across her ample chest. 'And anyway, he told me they never makes much outa squibs, unless it isn't won.' Bella stopped and waited for the sense to penetrate Nobbler. 'Aye, if it isn't won! He, he, he.'

Nobbler's shoulders began to shake with his mirth. He turned to Bella, grinning. He nodded his head in agreement and then went to his big chair. This occupied a space next to the secondary table in the living-room, and allowed a view through the living-room and along the passageway to the front door. That chair was most handy for anyone who wished to know what went on at the rear of the house – the view from the living-room window was reflected in Bella's press mirrors – and whoever called at the front door. Should Corrigan call, that chair was nearest the back door. Coppers in those times would never dream of sending another around the back. You had to catch your man red-handed, that is, if you really wanted to catch him?

Nobbler could sit quietly contemplating life in that chair. He had sight and sound of his pigeons from the backyard mingled with the contented clucking of his hens. He looked across to Bella from this strategic position.

'Ah think ah'll start a book without a pot, Bella! There's more money in thrupenny bets than sellin' squibs or runnin' for Stan!' Nobbler nodded his head to reassure himself that it was so.

Bella clapped her hands in agreement. At least she wasn't going to be the banker. Her money was safe. If Nobbler didn't win much, at least he wouldn't lose. She gave him a big smile.

'Aye lad, that's the way! Take yor thumb outa your mouth, you little tinker! Kettle's nearly on the boil, Tom, let's have a cup o' tea.'

He on the fender obeyed. It didn't do to oppose Grandma.

Nobbler's small coal

It was as Bella had predicted. Little apples are sweet apples. Small sure profit was better than large risky profit.

Nobbler had said it. 'It's like smaal coal, lass. It shovels better than them big lumps that rolls off yor shovel.' He was still working at the Gas Yard, five days a week. Still hawking coal around the district on Saturday with his son-in-law, Billie, Mrs. Billie's husband.

This coal round had been used in the past to collect bets for Stan Black. Now he was collecting for himself. A somehow much sweeter proposition. Why hadn't he thought of it before?

All his big bets, single big bets, from people suspected of having 'inside information', were layed off with Stan Black and other bigger bookies, through 'Our Robert or our

John,' as Bella had instructed. The youngins', Jos and Eddie, weren't allowed to take part in laying off, much to the chagrin of Jos, the one most likely to follow in his father's footsteps. Bella had other ideas for the youngins'.

Nobbler now had the Coke Works, the Gas Yard, some pubs, and pick-up points in various back lanes. Monday and Tuesday were bad days for pick-ups. Those days were usually washing days and the back lanes were festooned with clean washing stretched from wall to wall. The upstairs flats had high overhead pulley lines where washing could flap safely out of reach of coal-carrying carts. Many an angry word was exchanged between an irate lady and the horse rearing in panic at flapping sheets.

It was against the by-laws to block the back lanes with flapping sheets. It was also against the law to take bets. Mondays and Tuesdays called for great diplomacy.

He was taking in three pounds a week in thrupenny and sixpenny bets. More than he got as wages working in the Gas Yard. Three pounds a week, fat times indeed. Anything that looked like it came from somebody who had 'information', who staked up to five bob, was treated with great suspicion. It was debated but layed off with anybody who would take it. Any laid-off big bet that didn't win was treated with dismay. They would say, 'There'yar, that nag never had a chance. We shouldn't have layed it off.' It was, after all, worth many thrupenny or sixpenny bets.

Bella, though tempted, was still cautious. 'It's not worth the risk. You's get nee pot!'

It was true. Nobbler still had no pot. He wasn't one for saving. At the end of the year he should have been worth £150. He wasn't. Where had the money gone?

'Well, ah had to give a bit to Bob and a bit to our John, and there's our Jos and Eddie. Billie needs a bit for collectin'. Our Jane, she's always skint.' You had to be extremely self-centred to grow a pot. Nobbler had not that talent.

It was elevated living but it was hard work. Well, not exactly hard work. It was like, Nobbler had mused about it, 'Aye, it's like ah said before, it's like shovellin' that smaal coal. It sticks to yor shovel but it doesn't burn very well. It doesn't bring a lot of heat. Takin' it aal in aal, it's better than backin' losers.'

What wouldn't he give to have some real good nuts in place of that dull smaal coal which brought no fire to his life. There was no excitement in thrupenny bets. Is that what he really craved, this champion quoit player? The excitement of winning or losing?

Nobbler began to wonder why certain people betted every day. He had his regulars. He began to see he was once a similar and constant loser. Sometimes his regulars had a win and that win appeared to put a sparkle in their lives. He knew they must lose in the end, the odds always being in his favour. Were they, as Bella had called him, mugs?

He was often tempted to say to some well-worn, ill-clad lady with harassed look, clutching that slip of paper and perhaps her last thrupenny bit, 'Whey lass, keep your money for yor bairns. Don't you know you canna win?'

Would Bella have said, 'Yor too soft, Tom. You'll never make a business man!' She wouldn't have changed him for, 'that Scots buzzer, Carnegie!'

If there was no real elation about the small good profit from those thrupenny bets, Nobbler was still proud and pleased to be quoit champion. His pigeon cree, which sat upon the hen cree at yard level, had been given a new lease of life. Old leather-type hinges to the letting traps were replaced by brass types. The trellis adornment topping the cree was renewed and freshly painted. None of this deadened the noise made by twenty-five pigeons, five hens and one very noisy cockerel.

Pigeons, frowned upon when you were a mere punter, became more acceptable when you were a bookie; Bella's scowls became a mere grimace, should one of Tom's pigeons leave its mark on her as she made her daily journey across the backyard to the lavatory. A yard that had to be swilled with buckets of fresh water every day. Only the fresh eggs from the hens made the noise and the smell acceptable, but only just.

Nobbler now had the fastest pigeons in the district. Is that where some of his profit went? Buying the top breeders? You could win money with fast racing pigeons. You could be owner, trainer and jockey. You were the only one in possession of that vital 'information'. Inside information.

The back of Nobbler's house was easy to spot to his high fliers. The brick walls leading down to his pigeon cree were white-washed. Homing birds could easily pick out their loft from among the scores of back-to-back up and down flats in that district.

Tardy birds, wanting to socialize on backyard walls or roof tops, or in dangerous places where some prowling moggy might pounce, were encouraged to come home by Nobbler and his lads. The rattling of tin cans containing corn accompanied by shouts of, 'Ho-way, Ho-way, Ho-way, me beauties!' helped draw the homers closer to home.

They were agreeable times. The harmony dulled Nobbler to facts of life. He thought about giving up his job at the Gas Yard. He mused about making more money playing quoits and flying his pigeons. Bella was livid.

'What? You must be mad! You's got bairns to feed.'

'They's not bairns any more. Bob and Jane are married,' Tom reminded her.

'Aye, well, they'll have bairns. They'll need help. Many's the lad who would like yor job at the Gas Yard.'

Nobbler put his retirement plans from the Gas Yard in his pocket.

Nobbler ... Nobbled!

They'd been to Scarborough for a long weekend, Nobbler and Bella. The arms-folded-on-chest-nowt-to-do-brigade were waiting for them. The good news had travelled fast. Good news for some was bad news for Nobbler and Bella. The bold and brassy were on their front steps, the twitching front-room curtains hid the shy, or those in debt to Bella.

They sniffed when they passed, 'There she goes, Queen Victoria, you'd think she'd had a flush lav aal her life.'

The grim news was given by Annie the major-domo.

'There's a man here for his Saturday money. Our Robert and our John are nee where to be seen.' Our Annie waited until they were seated. Bella removed her big hat after pulling out those huge hat pins; barbs big enough to pin a man to the wall. When they were safely out of the way, Annie continued, ready to head for the door.

'He says he wants a hundred and fifty pund!' She made for the door. 'Ah'll go and get our Robert and John.'

Bella smoothed her hair. 'What did she say? Did she say,' the sense finally penetrated, 'A HUNDRED AND FIFTY PUND!' The windows rattled, the hens flew about the backyard, and the pigeons flew off to the nearby roofs. The observer on the fender hoping for rock from Scarborough took off after his Ma.

It was a full week before they were speaking again, Nobbler and Bella. She'd said every day, 'Ah knew this would happen. Them two young buggers, especially that John, he takes after you, not me.'

'Ah told him to back it off!' Nobbler reminded her.

'The bugger's like his father! Too bloody flighty! Just wait till ah get my hands on him!' Bella's wrath finally subsided but she never forgot that time when she had to draw out of 'The Store'. Her Co-op bank balance was left with a gaping hole that might never fill again. She would never ever forget that day she came back from Scarborough. John lived with Robert, Jane and Annie for a month before he dared show his face at Bella's house.

It was Billie, Annie's husband, who gave them the clue; perhaps John wasn't to blame after all.

'Poor lad didn't have time to back it off. The bet was put on at the last minute. He tried to put it on with Fergy, him on Reedheugh Road, but he was nee where to be seen.'

'There was Sales'y and Fenwick and the Boltons,' Bella snapped back. 'Stan's just up the lane.'

'And Buller Pervis,' Nobbler reminded. He looked keenly at Billie. 'You thinkin' what aahm thinkin', son?'

'John had nee time to back it off with the others before the Chronicle was oot! Neebody takes bets after the results are stamped in the stop press at Reedheugh Road.' Billie's eyes seemed to say, 'do you see what ah mean?'

'And neebody doon in this district sees the Chronicle for aboot ten to fifteen minutes.' Images began to mount in Nobbler. 'And our Jos could run from Reedheugh Road in one minute, ah'll bet.' Slim young Jos was fleet of foot.

'Gimitty Gawd!' Bella exclaimed. 'Whey y'bugger!' But it was Bella who wouldn't allow Jos to be used for laying off. Nobbler didn't press that point, but it was worth debating.

'Aye, ah'll bet our Jos could run to Reedheugh Road in one minute.'

'You and yor bettin'!' Bella snapped. 'Won't you ever larn? You's not doin' any more bettin'. Not with my money, so there!' It was a very sore subject. Her 'store book' lay like a coldstone in her money pockets. It froze with emptiness.

'Ah know somebody who can go faster than young Jos.' Billie's eyes twinkled with mischief.

Nobbler rose to that bait. Nobody could run faster than his son Jos. That was a fact. A fact he would back with money.

'Ah'll lay two to one neebody of the same age can beat wor Jos in shoes or bare feet!' He declared it with thumbs in waistcoat pockets standing in front of the fire.

'The question is, can he run from the Chronicle office in Newcastle, in one minute?' Billie's eyes retained that twinkle.

'Course he cannot! Don't be daft, lad, neebody could dee that!' Nobbler snorted. 'Taak with sense, lad!'

'Them racers out there, they could come back from the Chronicle office in one minute!' Billie pointed through the back window into the yard.

'Course they could! They's the fastest in the district,' Nobbler agreed, proudly.

Bella was about to condemn both of them. Consign both them and their wagering to the devil.

'Come to the point, lad, what's on yor mind?' Bella was getting interested. That store book beckoned attention. Was it beginning to warm up?

'If John was to take three fliers ower to Newcastle, we might get our-sels three winners, afore the Chronicle comes out in the Teams.'

'That's cheatin',' Nobbler exclaimed. He chortled at the thought.

'We's been cheated!' was Bella's answer to that. Was that store book gettin' warmer.

'If me calculations is correct,' said Billie, 'we could have aal of five minutes to play with. One minute for the bird to get to the yard and one more minute to coax him in with a hen bird. It might not work every time, but it will work.'

'Aye, our Jos could get to Stan and the Boltons and Sales'y in them other three minutes,' Nobbler reflected. 'But it's still cheatin'!'

'We's been cheated and this store book is empty!' Bella

waved her store book. 'And Miss Mulligan has a brother who works for the Chronicle.'

Somehow, the mere mention of that elegant lady's name put the stamp of approval on the scheme. And Miss Mulligan's brother, he was bound to help; it was a good business arrangement. As Billie pointed out, it was legitimate, it was 'inside information'. Everybody used that. Didn't the nobs do it?

And so it was. The syndicate was formed.

As Nobbler had said, 'It's a good job the Jews doesn't like pigeons. Bella was so mad when she had to pay out, she sold aal the hens to Killihen Jackson up the lane. She would have got rid of aal my top fliers as well if Killihen would take them. If the Jews liked pigeon pie, we'd have nee carrier sarvice between wor backyard and the Chronicle.'

They didn't bother with hens any more. The welfare of the pigeons was all-important.

Yes, it was true that Nobbler's pigeons could be released from Westgate Road and fly to his cree in his highly white-washed backyard in one minute, as long as they didn't stop to socialize with the pigeons on George Stephenson's statue.

They'd worked out a colour code of eight colours. Should the homing pigeon be tardy in lighting at the cree right away, they could read the colour on its leg if it dallied on the roof. Nobbler would take that responsibility with his little telescope. The coloured ribbons were bought by Bella at the 'Store'.

If it wasn't a perfect scheme, it was profitable. They'd decided, heavily advised by Bella, 'Nee daft bets! Nee pund bets at fifty to one. Just canny doubles with nee more than five bob on!' It was good advice from an expert who knew nowt about bettin'. So she said.

Nobbler bet every day, with thrupence or sixpence. He won or he lost. Just like the other mugs. On Saturday, he won three or four pounds. The hard bit, it was a unique sort of torture, was to ignore the horse that won at fifty to one. The threat of Bella's wrath however was enough to keep them under control.

He was only betting. If it was unlawful it wasn't as bad as 'runnin'' for one of the local bookies. Corrigan and Drummond had said so that New Year's Eve they appeared at Nobbler's annual shindig. If Corrigan was there, 'for a gargle', helmet in hand, he would exit on the appearance of Drummond. They would both disappear if they got 'the wire' that Sammy Chocolate, (the heed slop), was also making the rounds. It was a rowdy time of visiting and merry-making.

Thirty people could crowd into the two rooms and a scullery. The 'bairns' and the other lemonade drinkers occupied the front which used to be the shop. Bella had no need of a shop now. Not in her house. She was thinking of something on a grander scale. A shop on the Teams 'golden mile', Askew Road.

'That's how Stan started. He made a bit from his book and started his shop. We could dee the same.'

She would be in her usual place on New Year's Eve; her main cronies sat next to her. Her square table would have her best linen table-cloth, gleaming white. If that table was a platform for the week-end jug of best bitter, it became on that annual occasion an altar for the bottled offerings from the revelling New Year visitors. The other matriarchs who attended relied on those offerings for free refreshment.

The fender was parked elsewhere to prevent the happy jiggers from tripping over it into the fire. It didn't take much to bring a man down in those boozy hours.

The wafer-thin Sunday tea-set was packed away in Bella's back bedroom which was taboo to all except the major-domo, 'Our Annie'. Safe and away from the vibrating mass of happy humanity jigging as if possessed. The contents of Bella's press and sideboard jiggled in harmony to so many happy feet.

Sons Robert and John were usually the main performers. If they went too far with their drunken songs, Bella, if a bit tipsy herself, would soon call them to order.

All the matriarchs would sing their favourite song. Usually a mournful dirge. Should one be a bit quavery the others would help her along. All would join raucously in the chorus to help make Nobbler's party the noisiest in the street.

The major-domo would have cooked a huge ham in the set-pot to provide sandwiches galore. The set-pot then became a huge cauldron of New Year's Day soup from the stock stemming from the ham. That soup was famous as the only real remedy for New Year's hangover. Soup that was the only sustenance the boozers had to get them 'over the watter' to see the Magpies play.

Annie's soup, that great reviver, had no magic spell to cast away the gloom that fell on the household when they returned from the football match. It had been a wonderful but wearisome twenty-four hours. It was as if they had to pay for their enjoyment the hard way.

The lads had piled back into the house full of the match. Nobbler had gone to look at his pigeons. He returned, almost stumbling into the scullery. He was white-faced.

'They's aal deed!' he exclaimed to Bella; no one else mattered.

'What's aal deed? Who's deed? What's up, lad?' Bella didn't fancy laying anybody out just then.

'Me pigeons! They's aal deed!' He went back to the cree to check. Maybe he'd been dreaming.

The lads who had been clamouring for tea followed him out. Sure enough, there they were, Nobbler's pride and joy, silent and dead.

John pushed past his father and picked one up. Somebody had lit a candle so they could see better. In the light from that candle they could see the wound at the throat. He chose another. It was the same. Somebody said,

'Whey y'bugger!' They got a torch and shone the light around the cree. Silent birds lay all around. All thirty of them. Cocks and hens. Youngin's and champions.

'Been a ferret in there, Da!' John looked at his father and rushed out into the lane and the darkness to hide his tears.

There would have been another bit-of-a-booze-up that night. There was still plenty of soup and ham sandwiches and bottled refreshment. The soup was cold, the beer flat, the sandwiches tasted like sawdust, because the recipients felt the same.

It was work next day for those who had work. They could do their brooding there away from Bella. They brooded, she thought it out. There would be no Saturday bonus that week.

After work and a long, silent and solemn sit in his chair, he wanted to know. 'How could a ferret get in ma cree?' he was asking himself. 'Never heard of a ferret gettin' at pigeons.'

'Neebody around here has a ferret! If we was back at Hillgate, or if we was in the country, ah could understand it, but ah've never heard of a ferret in the Teams.' Bella rocked on her chair like a Jew at the Wailing Wall. She suddenly stopped her rocking as if that motion had brought understanding.

'Course, the quickest way to put us outa business, is for somebody to put a ferret in the cree when they knew we was oot!' She fired that at Nobbler.

Who knew they'd all be at the match over the watter? Everybody in the Teams, that's who.

'Didn't you hear owt, lass, when we was at the match?' Nobbler knew that was a forlorn hope. She'd already have said.

'Pigeons is always makin' a row. Besides, ah dozed off. We should have locked that back door.' So they should have but they never did. Not till night. They had no enemies, so they'd thought.

Nobbler spent a sleepless night pondering. The shock of losing his pride and joy was torture enough. But a deliberate slaughter? It was hard to accept. He just couldn't see anybody doing a thing like that. Acceptance was slow but it came.

Bella wasn't asleep when he made his decision. Nobbler stared up to the ceiling, not wanting to look through the window on his left, from which through the gloom could be seen the hump of his now empty cree.

'Ah've decided you is right, Bella! That ferret didn't get into ma cree by itsel! It was put in!'

Bella was some time in replying.

'Aye, aye, now you's only got to find out if it was Harry Thomas, Jack Kennedy, Bill Madox or Tom Pearson, them's the pigeon men. Then there's the bookies! Stan, the Boltons, Fergy, Sales'y, Fenwick, Buller Purvis.' She pulled the bedclothes up to her chin. 'Course, them's yor marras, Tom. They wouldn't do that to you, would they?'

Nobbler was stunned by that. What had he ever done to them? They wouldn't do a thing like that to him. Not to Nobbler. But somebody had!

He sat up suddenly in bed with clenched fists. His face took on that determined championship-class look.

'If ah thought any of them buggers '

'It's a sign, lad. A sign! Enough's, enough! Ah've got me money back, with a little interest. Let that be the finish. Nee more bettin', nee more worry. Gan to sleep, lad!'

PART TWO

Big Aunt Mary and Jinny the Seer

The matter of the ferret in the pigeon cree, if indeed it was a ferret that had killed Nobbler's pigeons, was not likely to be forgotten. Not by Nobbler. Bella's subjective signs meant little or nothing to him.

Bella had thrown enough names at him to confuse him. Stop Nobbler from going out with the lads to thump those they thought had put the ferret in the cree. She thought it prudent not to mention her visit to Jinny Barker. He might blow up at the mere mention of Jinny.

Jinny was the local fortune-teller. She lived right across the lane from Bella. Jinny was a bit fey. People either swore by her or at her. Nobbler hadn't a good word for her. He thought it rather odd that a lass as 'doon-to-earth as our Bella', who could see through tipsters like Ky-Wy, couldn't see through the fey Jinny.

'Keep away from that Jinny Barker!' he told whoever was in earshot and mostly for Bella's sake. 'She's daft! The way she looks at you, you'd think she wasn't here at aal!'

You could have a sixpenny reading with Jinny from the cards. You could have a card reading for a penny. Trouble was, for that level of fee, everything happened in a 'three'. You'd win, lose or die, in a 'three'. If you wanted a more down-to-earth prognosis, it would cost you five bob.

It was usually a visit from 'Big Aunt Mary' that sparked

a gathering in Bella's house. As many as ten would crowd around her big table with Big Aunt Mary interpreting everything Jinny conjured up.

Big Aunt Mary was as jolly as her girth. She came in a hire car; a hire car with a limp. It lost its limp when Big Aunt Mary alighted, was got out. Getting her out was a task in itself. Like prising a winkle out of its shell. She would shake like a huge jelly as Nobbler tried to pull her out. With the driver inside pushing, and Nobbler pulling, they would eventually get her out, to pleas of, 'Mind where yor puttin' yor hands, young fella, ah'll tell ma man on you.' The driver in some embarrassment would depart, sitting six inches lower than when he came. It was like delivering a huge barrel; a huge barrel of fun.

Big Aunt Mary got on well with everybody. She drank, swore and smoked like a man. 'Better than any man, hinny!' she would say. When Bella would say, 'Ee yor awful, our Mary,' Mary would counter with, 'Ah, yor too soft, our Bella! Why should them buggers have aal the fun?' She meant the menfolk.

If Bella was chief matriarch, she was nevertheless dimmed slightly by her big sister when she came to visit. Bella was glad to see her sister when she came and just as glad when she went. It could be a tiring day, Big Aunt Mary's day.

There would be questions, endless questions.

'How are you, Nobbler, then? What fettle? How's little Jane? What? Not again? And that big bugger not tippin' owt up? Ah'll dee for that bugger one of these days.' She would roll up her sleeves in preparation. She could lay out a man with one blow. Dead or alive, she'd laid men out.

It was the five-bob fee that brought the truth about Nobbler's pigeons; the truth as far as Bella was concerned. Jinny had read the cards and the teacups that day.

'The doves will fly no more!' she announced. 'I see a tall dark man with sharp white teeth.'

Aunt Mary took that in with popping eyes and a sharp intake of breath. She looked at Bella to see what she made of it.

'Did he have a fanny hat?' she enquired of Jinny. 'If he had a fanny hat, it'll be Big Dan for sure! Did he have a fanny hat, Jin?' The fee had been used up by that time.

It was when they'd had tea, then moved on to the 'best bitter' that Aunt Mary reached her peak. She could sing like an angel when she got tipsy, and when she was feeling good. She usually saw things in black or white, 'You's either a goodun' or a badun'.' Big Dan, little Jane's husband, him with the fanny hat, she had him marked for a villain. 'Ah'll swing for him!'

Bella, being ladylike, would drink from her own gill glass. Mary, when in full flow, would reach for the big jug. After ensuring the supply, 'Get yors, Bella, get yors, Tom,' she'd raise the jug to her mouth and take a slurp. It would be a good swig and a sign of a lively night. She did, after all, need more refreshment than others seeing she weighed twenty-two stone.

After that unladylike gulp and gasp of pleasure, she'd wipe her lips, hang on to her jug, and continue her harangue of that wayward husband. 'Aye, ah'll swing for that bugger one day.'

Bella would put the brake on that. If she welcomed Mary she, Bella, was still boss.

'Now then, our Mary, cause nee trouble. You canna come between man and wife. Ah've told our Tom the same. When a lass gets married, she's got to lie in the bed she's made for her-sel.' Bella resumed command. She very rarely got tipsy. There was no time that she left her property unguarded.

Nobbler had sat quiet. He would have liked to agree out loud with Mary, but he was a bit resentful; after all, disciplinary action of a son-in-law was his unwritten duty. But what could he do? A marriage in his eyes was, 'till death us do part!' If he didn't mind clouting Big Dan, he wouldn't want to 'swing' for him. But was it Big Dan who put the ferret in the pigeon cree? Ill-treating a daughter was one thing, and bad as it was, was it as bad as killing his pigeons, his real pride and joy? And in addition, there was the loss of his lucrative scheme. Yes, and the pigeons were harmless, unable to defend themselves, and young Jane had married that big boor of her own free will. A man had to weigh up all the pros and cons, pigeons now, they might be worth takin' that risk; if only he could be sure that it was Big Dan who put that ferret in with his pigeons. But he wouldn't risk swinging for it. He was the mainstay of his family, couldn't take that much risk, not even to get back at Big Dan. But you never know, one dark night, when he had a belly full of booze, Big Dan, big as he was, Nobbler stopped at musing what he just might do, on a dark night.

Nobbler's thoughts were interrupted as Big Aunt Mary hurtled on. He hoped she'd get to singin'. He liked to hear her sing. On the other hand, if she got too much to drink, she just might go out and look for Big Dan. Not that she'd find him; little Jane never could, and her with them three bairns to feed. Aunt Mary was singin', but not the right tune for Nobbler.

'When ma man comes in drunk from the docks with nee money, ah gives him a good bashin'!' Aunt Mary snorted into the jug. 'Y'just got to let the buggers know where their duty lies. It's bairns first with me! Bairns first and if there's owt left, aye well, a man's entitled to a drink and a smoke. Aye and so is his bloody wife!' This was delivered with a toss of her head and a swing of the jug.

'Ee, our Mary!' Bella protested. 'Aal men's not the same. My Tom '

'Aye, yor Tom's a goodin'. Ah know that he's not flaky. But there's them that is and is gettin' away with it.'

Nobbler had begun to resent this line of criticism. It began to look like a condemnation of himself. He would take that from nobody. It was Annie the major-domo who changed the subject.

'Give us a song, Aunt Mary! Sing, My wild Irish Rose! That's my favourite song.' Who could refuse the major-domo?

The hire car came to take Aunt Mary back to West Street. She was happy now and still singing. Nobbler and the lads trundled her along the passage to the street. The driver waited in trepidation and Aunt Mary greeted him with, 'There's me bonnie lad!' He had the anxiety of a lorry driver caring about his springs.

Bella stood on the step almost wringing her hands in anxiety.

'Ee, what will people think? You two lads, Jos and Eddie, you go with your Aunt Mary. See that she gets home alright. See her right to the door, mind.'

Amid cries of goodbye and calls of, 'Hoy oot! Hoy oot!' from the chasing children, the hire car took off for West Street. It was still with a limp despite Jos and Eddie as side ballast.

If he had not lost a lot of sleep since the loss of his prize pigeons, the matter still occupied Nobbler's mind. As he gazed at his empty cree and caught the enquiring glances of the lads, he knew something had to be done. They would expect it. The boss had to put matters right. But where would he start?

Revenge, if it did not fill his heart now, still had a place. Matters had to be balanced. It was true that Bella had her money back and a bit to spare. But he had no racing pigeons to gladden his heart. It would take time to build a prestigious flock.

He was still quoits champion but felt little pleasure in that. His head was still buzzing with suspect names. Harry Thomas, Jack Kennedy, Bill Madox, Tom Pearson; they were the pigeon men. Then there were the bookies; were they involved? If yes, which one? Was there more than one involved? Could it be Sales'y? Fergy? The Boltons? Buller Purvis, hm, could be his style.

Jack Kennedy and Bill Madox, and maybe Tom Pearson, they might be 'marras'. The bookies weren't marras, they were business rivals. They were the ones most likely to want to 'stop his tap'. But how could they know about the 'inside information' from the Chronicle office? It was a most puzzling situation.

Bella had said it was a 'sign'. How daft lasses could be. Everything had to be so mysterious. It was just plain jealousy. When you gets too good, the other buggers have to hold on to your shirt-tail to hold you back. And that Big Dan, he was another problem, couldn't let Big Mary take care of him; he wasn't her problem. That was a man's job; his job! But what about Big Dan? Did he have owt to do with the pigeons? Nobbler hadn't heard about that seance and the 'tall dark man with the sharp white teeth, who might have a 'fanny' hat'. But nevertheless, Big Dan was a flaky character; that was yet another name to add to his list.

Nature has a way of solving problems. One problem was about to be solved. A sudden yell from Bella brought him from his pondering.

'Tom, Tom, come quick! Big Dan is bashin' our Jane again!' Bella's cry for help reached out past Nobbler out to the lads in the lane. They ran in answer to that summons with their father, through the passageway into the street. Then up to their sister Jane's flat four doors away.

They gathered at the doorway. They could remember last time they'd done that. The door had been locked but they'd smashed their way in. They had found their sister Jane screaming blue murder and fighting off her brute of a husband. He was as drunk as ever. Six foot four and fifteen stones. They'd left him lying there in his own blood. Some of them were only half his weight. They took their sister and the bairns back to Bella's house. That had been six months ago!

This time their sister was at the open door, waiting. No

sign of the big man. No bashing this time. They stopped in wonderment, not knowing what to do.

'In there! In there!' Jane screamed. 'He's in there! Ah think he's deed!'

They raced in. They didn't know why. Reaction perhaps to save anybody, even Big Dan. They raced into the kitchen. Nobody there. They ran into the bedroom and there he was, the big man, terror of the neighbourhood, stretched out like a huge log. As dead as anybody could be.

They approached with caution; even reverence. After all, he was their brother-in-law.

'Is he deed?' Bob asked tremulously.

Nobbler went to take a closer look. It was an ill-lit room.

'Aye, he's deed! Deed alreet! The bugger's deed drunk! Take a good look, you lads. Take a good look and see what can happen to you when you's got a belly full of beer and faal asleep in a room where there's cockroaches. Take a good look. If that doesn't put you off yor beer, nowt will!'

The lads took a closer look, but Jos and Eddie backed off and ran to the door with sickening looks on their faces.

'It's the smell of the beer y'see,' Nobbler explained. 'Them little black buggers is attracted by the smell. It's meat and drink to them, a drunken man.' He proceeded to knock the hard-backed beetles off the big man, who'd not stirred.

The three, Nobbler and Bob and John, proceeded to stamp on the cockroaches.

'Pick the bugger up and put him on the bed,' Nobbler indicated.

'Leave the bugger there, da! Ah've been thinkin'. Bet he's the one who put the ferret in with the flyers?' Bob rumbled.

'Aye, and so he might be. But we've got nee proof. We always pays our debts, we Dobsons; but we's nee barbarians. Put the drunken bugger up on the bed and light the gas-light. Them little black buggers won't come out in the light.'

There was no arguing with the boss, so they lifted the big

man on to the bed out of the reach of those hard-backed beetles.

'Ugh!' John grimaced. 'There's one in his mouth.'

'Aye, take heed,' Nobbler grunted. 'This is one of life's lessons. When you's helpless your enemies can feed off you. Never get in that state. Ah wouldn't want that to happen to ma worst enemy.'

They searched and stamped on the beetles when they found them. Those little ugly black cannibals. The big man never stirred from his drunken stupor. He never knew the horrible death he'd just missed. Death by choking, by cockroach!

It was back to mother with the bairns again. Jane moved in with her brood. As Jos and Eddie said, 'You never know who you wake up with in this hoose!'

The big man woke twelve hours later. He bawled for his dinner after he'd discovered where he was. There was no skivvy to tend to his masculine needs so he smashed up the house and stalked out. It was good riddance to bad rubbish!

Jos's Fancy

Eddie Dobson, Bella's youngest son, gazed askance at his brother Jos. With foot on stool in the yard Jos was busy, very busy, polishing his shoes. A pair of well-worn shoes.

'What you polishin' yor shoes for?' enquired Eddie. An enquiry not out of place, considering that shoe polishing was not Jos's strong point.

'Nowt to do with you, our kid. Ma's always tellin' us to polish our shoes. You should get yors polished.'

That took some pondering. Should he too polish his shoes?

'But we's only goin' runnin' round the block. You don't have to polish yor shoes to do that?'

That was quite true. They didn't need to polish their shoes to just run around the block; shoes polished or un-polished weren't needed. All you needed, all they needed, was the will and the time and the energy. All of these they had.

There was plenty of time these days. No pigeons, though they had been promised they'd have a new flock to look after. No betting. No records for young Jos to break getting to Sales'y or one of the other bookies with a hot 'tip'. It was a boring time for young lads denied their usual excitement.

The excitement wondering which coloured ribbon would be on the messenger from the Chronicle office. The excitement trying to call the flyer in. The coyness of some flyers as they rattled the corn tin or flashed the hen bird at her mate. That was all gone. They were now just as ordinary as all the other lads in the street. It was tedious.

Big Dan had gone off, God knows where. He might be back. Yes, he would be back. When he was skint and his fair-weather friends deserted him, he'd come back to little Jane. He'd came back before for a real meal. A huge pot-pie filled with tatties and steak and black-pudding topped with a succulent crust. A glorious enticement for any hungry man.

Meanwhile, life was tedious for Jos and Eddie.

The cockroaches had been a bit of a problem. A problem to be solved if Jos and Eddie were to have their bed to themselves. Their big sister Jane wasn't going back home until 'them black-clocks is gone!'

Nobbler had a brilliant idea. It was so simple.

'We'll put a pint of best bitter in a shalla dish one night. The little black buggers will come oot when they smell the beer, and they'll faal inside and get deed drunk.'

'A pint o' best bitter?' Bella could hardly believe her ears. 'There's nee need to waste good beer on them little buggers.

A cupful will dee.'

They got a dozen of the 'little black buggers' in one night. Jos and Eddie got their bed back.

So to break the boredom they had organized races 'roond the big block'. Not the little block, up their street and down the next. That was too easy for Jos. He wanted a real test of speed and stamina.

They would start at the lamp, bottom of their street, and could run along Rose Street, up Tyne Road East, turn left at the Mart, along Reedheugh Road, turn right at the 'Reedheugh' down Askew Road – it was the fast bit – past the 'Reedheugh Pit', back to their street. It was about a mile. Jos could do that in three and a half minutes. In his bare feet!

But here he was, polishing his shoes. Hence Eddie's questions, 'What you polishin' yor shoes for? We's only runnin' round the block?'

What indeed was Jos polishing his shoes for? The weight of shoes was not likely to increase his fastest time.

'But you only polish yor shoes when you's goin' to the Mission, or seeing a tart?' It suddenly dawned on Eddie; it wasn't Sunday, so the polishing wasn't for the 'Mission'. So all that tarting up, it must be for a 'tart'. A sweet young thing?

Jos reddened slightly as Eddie hit the mark. He went on polishing.

'It's that reed-headed Sarah Fergeson. Her with the blue ribbon? Ah wondered why she's as many times down here to buy donkey-stone.' That was it, Eddie had guessed it. He grinned in derision. 'Yor daft, our kid!'

Eddie again looked at those well-polished shoes.

'Aye, that's the one!' He nodded as he thought it out further. 'That's her! Red, white and blue Fergie. A white face, reed hair and that blue ribbon!' And he wasn't finished. He had a further good look at those well-polished shoes.

'By, our kid, yor real crafty. Them's yor worst shoes. They's got nee soles in them. Ah can see yor twinkies. They looks good on top but ah can see they's got next to nee leather. They'll not slow you doon. By, yor as crafty as me ma!'

Jos grinned and said, 'That'll be the day!'

An authoritative voice from the scullery rapped out, 'Ah can hear you, our Jos!' Bella came to the door. 'And you keep away from that lass.' A finger came up. 'Mind, ah'm, warnin' you!'

'Why shouldn't the lad do a bit of sparkin!' Nobbler looked askance at Bella. 'Most lads dee a bit of courtin'. What's wrong with that? What you got against Fergie's lass?'

'Nowt! Nowt! She's a fine lass ah'm sure.' Bella's attitude suggested otherwise. 'But you never know what the tinkers get up to.'

Nobbler grinned. 'He doesn't know what it's all aboot yet. Are they left-footers?' That with raised eyebrows. Bella wasn't too keen on Catholics. He tried to balance the issue. 'Wor Annie's Billy is a Catholic. Well, a sort of Catholic. He doesn't go to church now. He's a collapsed Catholic, ah mean, he's a relapsed Catholic.'

'You mean he's a lapsed Catholic. That's like not payin' yor dues into the Christmas Club. Ah've got nowt against Catholics.' Bella sniffed.

'Is they Jews?'

'Not that ah know of.'

Nobbler was mystified. What was all the mystery about? Still, he knew Bella well enough. The lass's mother must be in debt to her. That would be it. Bella went cool on people who didn't pay.

'Her Ma's a slow payer, eh?' Nobbler grinned at Bella.

'Nowt to do with brass!'

'Is her Da a skinflint Methodist?'

Bella shook her head. 'How do ah know? What you

askin' all these questions for? You didn't ask that many questions when our Jane married that big waster, Dan?'

That put Nobbler down a bit. He protested. 'He seemed a fine figure of a young fella. He was in work, in the pit. He had good money. Takes a brave man to work doon the pit.'

So that was what it was about. Bella was being protective. She didn't want young Jos to end up like little Jane. Nobbler smiled; now he understood. Aye, the lads were growing up. He'd noticed Jos with that double-breasted waistcoat. He hadn't said anything in case it hurt Jos's feelings. He was becoming a bit of a dandy, and only sixteen.

Nobbler was indebted to young Jos. His unstinting loyalty in placing those fast bets wouldn't be forgotten. If Bella thought it was a bit too early for Jos to go courtin', aye, still, little Jane was havin' a hell of a life. Bella didn't want Jos to end up the same way. Now he understood what it was all about.

'Aye lass, yor right!' Nobbler sighed. 'Aye, when you gets married, it's for good, that's to say, it's supposed to be for good, but you got to take the bad alang with it. But there's nee reason why it should be aal bad. Life can be hell with the wrang man or the wrang lass.'

Bella had sat in her chair with arms clasped around her middle; her pondering position. She smiled, at last she was getting through to Tom.

'You tell our Jos he's not to see that young tart again, Tom?' It was a suggestion. A suggestion that raised doubts.

Nobbler got up from his chair and stretched a bit. He gave Bella a bit of a grin; a weak grin.

'You tell him, Bella! It's you that doesn't want him to see the lass. You did say she was a fine lass? ... If ah tell him, he'll want to know why, and ah don't know why, do ah?' Nobbler gave Bella a little nod and went out into the yard. Bella knew what that little nod meant. It meant, over to you, Bella.

He didn't get far. Bella was up from her chair and bellowing as only Big Aunt Mary could bellow. It must have been in the blood.

'Nobbler! Tom! You come back in here!'

Even Nobbler, the boss, couldn't ignore such imperious command. He came back into the living-room as Bella resumed her throne. He took his place in front of the fire and stood there, thumbs hooked in his waistcoat pockets.

He gave Bella a look of exasperation. She was taking this protective business too far; in his opinion.

'Aye, so they's not left-footers? They's not Jews? They's not Methodists? Are they from South Shields, where the darkies come from? Does he drink in the "Coffin"?'

People who 'boozed' in the 'Coffin' wasn't in her zone of influence and therefore inferior.

Still Bella hesitated. What was it, how had the Fergesons erred?

'Well, if they's not any of them, what the hell is they?' His tone of voice showed he was fast losing patience.

The hesitation was still evident. Bella looked around to see if there was anybody in earshot. To reinforce this she arose and went to the back door. After looking out she closed the door. She returned to the living-room and inspected the passageway. There was no-one there but she closed that door also.

Only when she was sure they were alone did she come close to Tom. When people were around she never came close to Tom. She went closer and whispered in his ear.

'Her Ma and her, they have the same Da!'

A puzzled expression flitted across Tom's face. He had trouble working that out. He spoke at last after Bella had resumed her seat.

'How can her Ma and her have the same Da? That's daft!' The firelight at his back placed his face in shadow and hid his embarrassed thoughts.

Bella nodded, to reinforce her initial statement.

'But that's daft!' Nobbler insisted.

'Her and her Ma, have the same Da! Her Da's her Granda!' Bella insisted.

It took some time for the sense to sink in. Nobbler walked a simple straight path through life and deviations hardly occurred. The awful truth fell on him at last.

'You mean, you mean he's been stridin' his own doughter?' He got it out at last. He was almost afraid to say it. Even to his wife.

Bella nodded, red in face. You didn't usually talk directly about things of that nature in her world. A world of hints and nods.

Nobbler stared at her in disbelief. He was still questioning it. Somehow, it couldn't be true. But it was. He knew when Bella was at her most sincere.

'A fella stridin' his own doughter, well ah never. Why y'bugger! Why the dirty sod! HEY! OUR JOS!' Nobbler was opening the back door now. 'You come in here!'

Jos and Eddie were in the lane, resting from that run round the long block. They were aroused by that majestic command. They looked at each other. Was Big Dan back? They raced to their father.

'Aye, what's up Da! Is Big Dan back?'

Nobbler cooled. 'Na! Na! It's alright! It's young Jos ah want. You go and play, lad!' This to Eddie.

'Ah'll take it, if it's a bet you want?' Eddie was anxious to please.

'Na! Na! Nee bets, lad. Yor Ma wants to talk to our Jos. You go and play and our Jos'll be back in a minute.'

Jos came into the living-room in dismay. The tone of his Da's voice heralded some displeasure. What had he done wrong? His mind raced to his past indiscretions.

'Aye, Da? Aye, Ma? What's up?' Jos asked, coming into the presence.

'Sit down, lad!' Nobbler indicated his chair. That was threat in itself. Jos guessed he wasn't going to enjoy this. He sat down, wonderingly.

Nobbler and Bella stared at their son. He sat waiting; waiting for the accusation. Nobbler, with back to fire, looked at Jos, looked at Bella. Bella stared away from them both. She'd have gone out, if she'd dared. This was man's talk and therefore not for her.

'Aye, Da?' Jos decided to get it over with. Was it because he'd let the gallawa run off? Because they'd heard he'd punched Arthur Hazel? Had Sister Winnie been round from the Mission?

'Er,' Nobbler looked at the floor for inspiration. A deadly hush followed. What can you say to a 'youngin'' on a subject that you and your wife speak about only in whispers.

'Er.' Something had to be said. Nobbler began to sweat. He just couldn't say it. Not to his lad.

'Er, aye, we was just thinkin', me and yor Ma, wasn't we, Bella?' He looked at Bella and then at the floor for inspiration. He got it!

'Aye, we was just thinkin', it's about time you had a new pair of shoes. Them you've got on, they's almost wore out. Haven't they, Bella?'

Bella also took the easy way out. If it was hard for Tom, it was impossible for her.

'Aye, that's reet, lad. You need a new pair of shoes!'

Jos beamed. That was good news; no ticking-off and a new pair of shoes as well.

'Will our Eddie get a new pair as well?' he enquired.

'Aye, ah suppose so,' Bella almost groaned. It was turning out to be an expensive time, this sparkin' time.

Jos leaped up to tell Eddie the good news. He'd be even more popular with red, white and blue Fergie now.

Nobbler put his hands behind his back and warmed them at the fire. He needed a bit of a warm after that trying time. He didn't feel too bad about dodging the issue. After all, Bella could be wrong?

'You did say she was a fine lass? And after aal, lass, Jos'll have a fancy for more than one, if ah know him. Aye, and that Sister Winnie, didn't she say that we aal had the same faather. Looks to me like we's aal in the same boat, lass!'

There was only a snort from Bella as her answer to that.

Big Aunt Mary in the Clink

Weddings always gave everybody a lift. They needed a lift now.

The building of the cree and the acquisition of the fast flyers had been the culmination of many years' work. That did not come easy. Real work for real money was earned, in the pits, at the Gas Works, or the Coke Works, or the Coal Staithes, or perhaps the big Armstrong's factory. None of these occupations were likely to leave much energy for any strenuous pastime. This was the real bitterness, the loss of their precious effort.

Bella had said it was a sign. 'A judgement on us!' She wanted no more of it.

But the mystery had been created and it was a cloud on Nobbler's mind. The two elder lads, now men and both married, were still searching for clues as to who that mystery man was. If they found him, God help him! Bob and John could be very unruly, as Big Dan had discovered.

It was at Lizzie's wedding that the gossip started up again. Everybody was there. They even expected Big Dan to turn up for free booze.

'Mind, if he does, ah wants nee trouble. You know what drink does to the lads, and you too, our Tom. Ah'm warnin' you aal, nee trouble!'

Big Aunt Mary was in the thick of it, as usual.

'Maybe if yor lads forgot aal about them shit machines

and set their minds on another scheme, straight or under the table, they might have built an empire be now. The Gateshead Empire.' Aunt Mary guffawed and Bella giggled her tipsy giggle.

'Ee, our Mary, you mind your language, there's bairns here. Aye, if only they would, forget about them pigeons. Them pigeons is between them and their wits!'

The Dobsons' weddings were like a football match with no referee. That is to say, the referee was there but never moved from one spot. All the play had to come to her, Bella. She could send you off the pitch if you were less than perfect. As long as you acted perfectly in her limited range, you were alright to do as you pleased.

The matriarchs gathered around the Queen and songs were sung. It was like New Year's Eve all over again. But Bella would worry every minute she was away from home. The major-domo would be instructed to see that everything was locked and barred till Bella returned home for that last farewell drink with her cronies. Big Aunt Mary would stay all night.

As the celebrations wore the day and night away, the old gossip and fables would emerge. Everybody not present would receive a character analysis.

Any language considered to be too rough or bawdy by the referee would be censored with remarks such as, 'Mind yor tongue you!' or 'You shut up, you show me up!' or, 'Do you think so, hinny?' or, 'Ee, our Mary, there's bairns here!' The depth of blue pencil depending on your status.

Little observers, tucked away in some corner or under a table, might be greeted by, 'You little tinker, you shouldn't be here. Get yorsel in among the other bairns.'

'Ee, yor Lizzie looked loverly at the Church! And she's got a good strappin' fella. They make a good-lookin' pair.' Congratulations poured in measure with the drink.

'Aye, that's what they said aboot little Jane and that bugger Dan! Look what he turned oot to be,' Big Aunt

Mary snorted. 'And him not tippin' owt up yet, aal them poor bairns. Ah'd geld aal them buggers that went off and left bairns to starve.'

'It's a bit late to dee that!' Nobbler observed. 'Youngin's gets married when they has nowt. They's skint when they start and skint for the rest of their lives. The bairns come like buds on a tree every spring. They larns too late!'

'Yor not stickin' up for that big sod, are yer?' Aunt Mary was aghast.

'Ah'm only sayin', fellas is tempted into places they got nee brass for. If lasses didn't paint their gobs with reed paint they paint their gobs reed for a purpose. They's not so daft. They know what it's aal aboot!'

Bella was scandalized at that. 'Ah never painted my go – mouth!' She looked at Tom as if he was Benedict Arnold.

'Ah don't mean you, Bella!' Nobbler hastened to pacify her. 'Ah mean these youngin's. Ah don't know what the world is comin' to. What with fellas stridin' their ...' He wasn't allowed to finish.

'You shut up!' It was delivered like a rifle bullet. Bella smiled. 'You was sayin', Mary?'

'Aye, Bella, ah was just thinkin'. It takes you back. Who would believe ah was as skinny as yor Lizzie when ah was her age? Aye, my man was a strappin' young fella, just like yor Lizzie's, just look at us now.' A tear would appear. 'Ah was a beauty in my day. When ah was married ah was slim and a beauty, and Joe, he was a handsome lad.' A vivid description of her wedding would follow. She would be saddened, then start to sing. Sing sad songs. Beautiful sad songs you would never believe could come from such a rude lady.

All the matriarchs would weep and they too would join in. But the one who could make them weep, could also make them laugh. Laugh till they wet themselves.

'Ah mind that time when ah was here before. Was it yor John's weddin' or was it yor Bob's? No, ah tell a lie, it was yor Little Jane's weddin'. We was just sittin' here.' Aunt Mary laughed and had yet another sip. 'Havin' a little drinky and then yor Annie came rushin' in, aye, it would be yor Jane's weddin' cause yor Annie wasn't married then, anyway, she came rushin' in to say that Mrs. Wakenshaw was havin' another bairn and in her passage. What a funny place to have a bairn?'

Bella said, 'Aye, aye that's reet!'

'Aye, and you and me rushed up and there she was, poor lass; sittin' in the passage havin' the bairn, and the poor lass had her best hat on, well, ah ask you, you couldn't dee owt else but laugh, and it was nee laughin' matter.'

'Aye, she was in a terrible state,' Bella agreed.

'We shut the front door to keep the kids out. We cleaned her up and swilled the passage out but she kept shoutin' for her man. What's the use of them buggers at times like them?'

There were murmurs of sympathy. Yes indeed, what good were men.

'But she kept shoutin' for her man and ah thought he might be in another room, hidin' his-sel; that's what some of them dee instead of makin' their-sels useful. So ah went into the little bedroom at the back, and there he was, the poor sod had topped his-sel. He was a right old mess, blood aa'll ower the place; he'd made a bad job of it.'

'Ee, it was awful,' Bella agreed.

'Aye, the poor bugger was still makin' gurglin' noises. Blood aa'll ower his throat and shirt front. So what can you dee? So ah put him on the bed and put his feet on the bed-heed, he had his new beuts on. Ah thought it would be a pity to get them aa'll covered in blood, and there was that newish lookin' clippy mat, a pity to spoil that.'

'Aye, it takes aa'll of three weshin's to get blood oot of a clippy mat.' Bella agreed with that action.

'So as ah say, ah put the poor lad's beuts ower the bed-heed and left him lyin' there like a kosher pig. Aa'll the blood was soaked up by the bedclaes. Ah shut the door to keep the bairns oot. Best not to let them see him like that.'

'A kosher pig?' Nobbler questioned that. 'Killihen and them other Jews doesn't eat pork, Mary.'

Bella agreed. 'Nee such thing as a kosher pig. You can have a kosher chicken or a kosher coow, but there's nee such thing as a kosher pig.'

'Aye well, that's the way he looked to me, a bleedin' pig. He wasn't a Jew, was he? So it wouldn't matter which way up he was, poor bugger! Them Wakenshaws must have been in real trouble. The piss-pot was filled to the brim and looked like it hadn't been emptied for a week. What a pong!' Aunt Mary wrinkled her nose as she remembered that odour.

'You should say, chamber pot, our Mary!' Bella chided her sister.

'Aye, that's reet, our Bella, the chamber pot was filled with piss to the brim! God rest that poor lad's soul. We sent yor Annie to the station for Corrigan. They's never there when they's needed, them slops!'

They'd been talked out and worn out by Aunt Mary. She could go on forever, so it seemed.

Came the next day and it was soon time for her to return to the bosom of her own family. The exercise of getting her into the hire car began with the usual banter, Jos and Eddie again acting as side ballast. Off they went with children in hot pursuit; Aunt Mary might oblige by throwing out a few pennies in reward.

With the car springs bottoming all the way to West Street and the driver in constant anxiety should he have a puncture, they eventually arrived at Aunt Mary's place.

The unloading of the lady began amid more banter, with she having a 'bit crack' with the driver about special rates for special jobs. There was nothing ordinary about Aunt Mary. After threatening to 'clip his lugs' for his cheek, the driver went off to tell his mates his fisherman's story. No doubt Aunt Mary's twenty-two stones would grow to thirty or forty with the telling.

'C'mon in, lads!' Aunt Mary ushered her two nephews into her house. 'We'll have a cup of tea to recover. Ah hate them motor cars.' No doubt hers would be fortified with, 'just a nip'.

They'd just sat down to sip their tea and munch their biscuits when the front door opened and Aunt Mary's eldest daughter Tammie walked in. Aunt Mary greeted that entrance with enquiring eyes and pursed lips.

'Neebody here when yor Ma comes home. Where you been, lady?'

Jos and Eddie eyed each other. This domestic scene wasn't theirs. They'd feel much more at ease back on their own stamping ground, playing football. They were used to a daily stiff dose of ball practice, without which they could turn irritable. They gulped down their tea and prepared to leave. The conversation that transpired caused them to tarry awhile.

'Been down to the Sasaparilla shop, doon the High Street with Betty Robinson.' Tammie kept space between herself and her mother.

'Oh! Just to the Sasaparilla shop? You sure?'

Perhaps to reduce the suspicious pressure, to put the spotlight elsewhere, Tammie said, idly twisting strands of hair with her finger, 'Saw that Big Dan you're always on aboot.' She awaited the outcome.

'What?' Aunt Mary's hackles rose. 'You saw Big Dan, in the Sasaparilla shop?' That was unbelievable.

'Well, not exactly in the Sasaparilla shop. It was like this; Betty didn't like the sasaparilla. She said it left a funny taste in her mouth, so ...'

'So she thought she'd call into a pub to get the taste out of her mouth, and you went with her?' Aunt Mary's sarcasm was as thick as her tea. She'd heard it all before.

'Ah've told you, lady, you's too young to be goin' in

pubs! So what pub did you go in, not that bloody Castle?' She saw by the look on her daughter's face, it was the Castle.

What was so interestingly forbidden about the Castle? The two lads craned to hear.

'Aye, it was the Castle.' It came tearfully.

'The Castle! That bloody knockin' – She remembered she was in the presence of mere 'bairns'. She checked herself in time.

'Ah've told you to stay out of pubs. Especially that one!'

'Big Dan was there, with a bull's mate!' That also was a statement aimed at shifting that spotlight. It did and it didn't.

Aunt Mary jumped to her feet like a boxer rising to the sound of the starting bell.

'With a, bull's mate? How come you knows words like that, you little hussy?'

Tammie backed off. She thought she'd done the right thing offering that description. She knew other terms for a 'lady of the night'. She also knew if she used those other terms, she'd get a clout.

'He's in there, large as life, and she's painted like a tramcar. He'll have nowt left the way he's chuckin' his money aboot!'

That scored a direct hit. Big Dan was chuckin' away the bairns' money. Spendin' money on a painted hussy. It didn't bear thinking about.

'Where's St. Colman's Crozier?' She stalked to the lobby and took down a hefty stick lying on two horizontal pegs on the wall. It was a shillalah.

'See this,' she said to the two now highly interested footballers. 'This is St. Colman's Crozier, it has the power to return bairns' money back to bairns. Just you watch!'

Just you watch? Try and drive them away. This was far more interesting than football. Big Aunt Mary in full battle array. Those young eyes gleamed at the thought. What a story to tell. What a scene to brag about. It was short-lived.

'On second thoughts, ah think you two lads better go

back home. Aye, go back home and tell yor Ma and Da, ah'm sendin' their son-in-law back home. Home to work for his bairns.'

Tammie fed more fuel to the fire. 'She's wearin' them silk stockin's!' she said, mostly to the two lads. 'Ah could see her knees!' And, wistfully, 'She is real pretty.'

By that time Aunt Mary's crozier was marching down West Street to do it's duty. It was wrapped in a huge black shawl and twenty two stones of very angry lady.

The Castle was only a hundred yards away, downhill. Aunt Mary's majestic presence swept all aside as she waddled to her target.

It was Corrigan who brought the bad news. He came to the front door and waited. The jungle drums had already warned Nobbler so he was ready for him. He went to the open door and greeted Corrigan. The street was alive with eyes and ears.

'Wha'cheer, Bill! What fettle?' Nobbler greeted Corrigan.

'Ah've some bad news, Nobbler! Yor sister Mary, they's got her in Swinburne Street!'

In Swinburne Street? There was only one place of note in Swinburne Street, the main Police Station.

Bella pushed passed Tom. 'In Swinburne Street, what's she deein there? What's she done?' It was a fierce thrust.

'Ee, it's nowt to dee with me, missus,' Corrigan hastened to protest his innocence. 'They's phoned to us to tell you. She's alright though, but there's a charge agin her, it's disorderly conduct. She'll be up in Court next week!'

Bella went back inside and collapsed on her chair. 'Ee, the shame of it aal!'

Nobbler did the honourable thing.

'Will you come inside and have a drink, Bill?'

'Ah'd like to, Nobbler, but the way things are, some other time, eh?' Corrigan gave Nobbler a salute and went off.

Nobbler went inside again to be greeted by ...

'There'yar Da, told you that Big Aunt Mary was goin' to murder Big Dan. You should have seen the stick she had. Tammie says it came aal the way from Ireland. Here's our Eddie now, ah beat him by three minutes.' Eddie came panting in.

'Just saw Corrigan, at the front door, what did he want?'

'Go on, son, you was sayin', before Corrigan came?' Nobbler wanted more about Big Dan from Jos.

'Aye, as ah was sayin', Da, when wor Eddie and me got to the Castle ...'

'The Castle? That bloody den of iniquity!' Bella rumbled. 'What was you doin' there?'

'We was followin' Big Aunt Mary. You should have been there, Da, the folks runnin' and jumpin' aal ower the place. Big Aunt Mary cleared the whole bar. We could hear glasses and bottles bein' smashed in hundreds. You should have seen the lasses. Like Tammie says, they was painted like tramcars. And then the slops came, and then the Black Maria.' Jos's eyes widened in wonder. 'It was just like in the Police Gazette!'

Eddie said, 'Aye, that's reet, Da!'

Bella said, 'Ee, the shame of it aal!'

PART THREE

The 'Bud'

'Mary Ellen Maddox, you are charged, that on May the first, last, you did enter the premises of–' the Clerk of the Court wrinkled his nose in some secret disgust – 'the premises known as the Castle, and there conducted yourself in a disorderly manner.'

'Missus Mary Ellen Maddox!' said Aunt Mary, her hands clasped as if about to give a song.

'What's that?' the Magistrate enquired from his slightly elevated position. He occupied the middle one of the three seats, the others being vacant.

'She says she is a Missus, your Honour. Oh, you mean the Castle?' The Clerk thought that everyone had heard of the Castle. 'It's a public house, your Honour, of ill repute.'

'It's not! We sarves the best draught beer in the North!' The landlord was present and protested strongly.

'Silence in Court!' the usher shouted.

'How do you plead?' The Magistrate looked over his spectacles in the direction of Aunt Mary. She had nothing to say.

The Clerk took up the matter. 'How do you plead, Mrs. Maddox? Are you guilty or not guilty?'

'Ah was only gettin' money for the bairns.' Aunt Mary gave that heavy black shawl a heft further on to her shoulders. A homely chain-mail stitch which could fend off the world.

'You're in the Salvation Army?' enquired the Magistrate.

'Me, in the Sally Anne? Not me! Ah'm chapel, when ah'm there that is.'

'But you was at this place collecting for children.'

'Aye, for the bairns. Wor Jane's bairns.'

'I think there was an altercation, sir.' The Clerk got the case moving.

'I think Mrs. Maddox had better plead not guilty!' the Magistrate indicated to the Clerk who then committed the plea to paper.

The Magistrate leaned forward and tried to generate confidence to the accused.

'Tell us in your own words, er, Mrs. Maddox, what happened at this place called the Castle.' He beamed, or tried to.

'Well, yor Honour, ah went there to get money for our Jane's bairns.'

The Clerk muttered, 'We've heard that already.' The Magistrate waved him quiet.

'Did you go around the place with a receptacle? Were you invited. Did you ask for permission?' The eyes and specs sought an answer.

'Ah only had ma shawl and the bud. Big Dan was there. He had the bairns' money. Ah didn't ask anybody else but him.'

Bud, shawl and Big Dan? That took a bit of understanding. The Magistrate looked down at the Clerk. He had no clue to offer.

'This Big Dan, person. I suppose he is a person? Who is he and how does he fit into this?' he asked the Clerk.

The Clerk had a whispered discussion with a policeman.

'Er, we think this Big Dan person is in hospital, sir.'

'Then obviously he cannot appear as a witness. Are there any more witnesses?'

'There's the landlord of the public house, sir.'

'Put him up!'

The landlord took the oath. He promised to tell the truth, the whole truth, and nothing but the truth.

Aunt Mary's mouth opened wide in some amazement. The landlord didn't get to say a word.

'Him tell the truth? Nowt but the truth? Then let the bugger tell us where his wife is. His poor wife and four kids he deserted in Hillgate six years ago. Go on, Jack Spoors, tell us!'

'Are you suggesting that this witness is unreliable?' The Magistrate lowered the pen he had poised to take the testimony.

The black shawl simmered like tar on the boil.

'Unreliable?' The dock shivered under the pressure. 'Ask the bugger why he was sacked from the Moulders Arms back in Hillgate six years ago. Aye, then after that, ask him why he got the boot from the Askew Arms three years ago. Unreliable, huh, if you want a bent fiddler and a good beer stretcher, he's yor man.' She snorted like a hippo.

'Mrs. Maddox is suggesting that this witness is unreliable. Is he tainted?' This to the Clerk and the policeman. 'Were you sacked from these two positions as Mrs. Maddox suggests?' This to the now hapless landlord who had cringed under Aunt Mary's broadside. He nodded his head in the affirmative.

'You may stand down!' The legal pen pointed the landlord off the pitch. 'Are there any more witnesses?'

There was a hurried further discussion between the Clerk and the policeman. The main prosecution witness was destroyed.

'There is a weapon, sir. Er, an offensive weapon carried by the accused, er, in a disorderly manner?' The Clerk saw immediately he'd made a blunder. But would the Magistrate see it? He did.

'Can an allegedly offensive weapon be carried in a disorderly fashion?' The Magistrate raised his eyebrows, focusing on the Clerk. He baulked at the question. Charges had to be correct. Mixed charges erected legal problems.

Aunt Mary got him out of that corner.

'If yor talkin' about ma man's shillalah, it's nee offensive thing. It's a bud from St. Colman's Crozier; it can dee nee harm to any soul. It can only dee good; it got five quid for the bairns!' There was triumph in Aunt Mary's voice.

The Magistrate took that in with his usual reserve. After all, he'd heard queerer stories. The Court lapsed into silence, a silence punctured by a titter. The usher glared in its direction.

The Magistrate indicated to the policeman holding the shillalah. 'Bring that mysterious object to the bench.' It was duly handed up to him. He held the nobbly oak stick in both hands, the heavy end of which could crack an elephant's skull.

The Magistrate looked up at the assembly.

'I can see that this, er, stick, has nothing whatsoever to do with this charge. This is just an old person's staff. I find Mrs. Maddox not guilty!'

A voice in the body of the Court sounded, 'Ah should bloody well think so!'

'Silence in Court!' called the usher.

The silence that followed was a smooth bed for the next plaintive voice. 'Ee, the shame of it aal, wor Mary!'

Perhaps it will never be known if it was Aunt Mary who put Big Dan in hospital; whether the heavy end of the 'bud' from St. Colman's Crozier had connected with his skull and laid him out. Aunt Mary never said. One rogue's head was as good as the next to her.

Others then at the Castle that day might have said Big Dan was hospitalized because he dived through the nearest window trying to escape the fury that bore down on him.

The landlord behind the bar was the first to see Aunt Mary burst through his doors with her shillalah at the ready. Ready for any opposition.

He made three quick guesses. This irate woman was looking for her wayward husband; a common occurrence. She was a mother seeking her straying daughter. Or, his conscience oscillated ... she just might be looking for him. He held up one hand and then the other as if to ward off this vengeful body.

'We wants nee trouble, missus! This is a respectable bar. We wants nee trouble now!' His words had as much effect as trying to light a candle in a hurricane.

There he was, that Big Dan the waster! Chattin' up that painted bitch! Her with her skirt ower her knees! Aunt Mary took the shortest route to Big Dan's table, the tables and occupants in between swept aside like chaff in a high wind.

The young bitch – 'Ah gave her a wack on her arse for her cheek! – ran screaming for her life.' Big Dan made his escape the quickest way he knew how, leaving his cash behind. Aunt Mary picked it up. Nobody interfered. It was not uncommon for a lady to chase her husband out of the Castle.

That 'bud' from St. Colman's Crozier, that with the power to get money for bairns, was laid reverendly back on its pegs, on the hatstand in the hall in Aunt Mary's house. Would it ever have to be used again?

Short Back and Sides, Sir?

It took some time for the hubbub about 'the battle at the Castle' to die down. Jos and Eddie, they were there and saw everything, so they claimed. They never saw anything more than the blurring pandemonium everyone else saw, but they had vivid imaginations.

'She laid ten of them out, nee bother!' Jos exclaimed with

bloodthirsty glee. 'There was twenty or thirty of them. They aal run for their lives from Big Aunt Mary.'

Or was it simply that there'd been a number of guilty husbands there that day, trying to escape the limelight?

But those stories palled. Especially when there was inconsistancy. New adventures were needed to fill the gap left by the lost excitement of those profitable messengers from the Chronicle office.

Jos was getting taller and stronger. Eddie was shorter, more pugnacious; a strong lad. Jos would always be a 'slim Jim', quick to move and easy to please. He took after brother John. Eddie after Bob, so it was agreed.

Jos was to become an apprentice. To enter the 'hairdressing' trade.

'Bloody barber, that's what! The buggers has always got to have a fancy name for common or garden things. It's a good groundin' though. Keep him off the streets, away from the likes of Big Dan,' Nobbler rumbled.

'Aye, it might keep him oot the hands of the bookies. Ah thinks he takes after you. Wor Eddie, he's more like me. He's more settled like; looks after his money.' Bella had it all worked out. 'Aye, wor Jos takes after you. He's got an eye for horses and the lasses, just like you, Tom.'

Nobbler grinned at that. There was no escaping that eagle eye. 'Aye, wor Jos's a real flyer. They say he'll make a first class left-winger. Wor Eddie, he's more like a centre-half. He might score nee goals, but we can rely on him.'

The two young lads, they were the centre of focus now. All the others were married and settled, or unsettled, in their own homes. 'They's made their beds, they has to lie in them!' That was Bella's philosophy.

Young Jos could fast-walk to the Central Hairdressing Salon, beside the Central Station in Newcastle, in ten minutes. He'd clocked himself. It took him a minute longer on 'Mart' days. The cattle market was at the entrance to

Redheugh Bridge. On certain days it could be choked with traffic from the adjacent cattle pens.

He was now a 'hairdresser', well, he would clean up and make the tea. Be the local runner to the nearby bookie. He'd do that till he could be trusted to cut hair and shave a man with some confidence. He soon picked up the patter, 'Short back and sides, sir? Anything on, sir? Nice weather, sir?'

The Central Hairdressing Salon was just across the road from the Chronicle office. That office of 'inside information'.

Did a plaintive voice say, 'Pity wor Jos couldn't run a bit faster. He might have run us a few winners. Just to put a bit of jam on our bread.' Bella now had three more mouths to feed. Her sister Nellie had died leaving three teenage daughters to fend for themselves. They wouldn't have to do that with Aunt Bella around. Had hard necessity replaced caution?

'It wouldn't dee any good, even if Jos could run faster!' Nobbler had said so. He was back 'runnin' ' for Stan. Getting his small commission, and losing it trying to make it more. The mug's game.

'Aye, as you was sayin', Tom, it would dee nee good even if wor Jos ran aal the way. He's fast, but not as fast as a pigeon.' It was a pioneering remark. A mere matter of interest, not research.

'Naa lass, aal the bets has to be put in a bag these days. Bookies trusts neebody. There's a clock on the bag. Aal bets has to be locked in the bag afore the race; maybe a minute or two after the time, but only a minute or two. Nee chance there! Nee chance for inside information.'

That wasn't good news. No room for innovation. No room for craft or skill. What was the world coming to?

'Afore the first race, or the last?'

'Eh?' That caused those mental wheels to go round. By, that Bella was a crafty lass. She took the matter further.

'When you close that bag, what time does you close it? The first or the last race?'

'Well, we couldn't close the bag for the first race, could we? Stan would make nee profit. He works on the whole day.'

'So, if we had a mind, we could get some of that inside information, on the first and second races, afore you closed that bag? Ah was only funnin', Tom.' Bella's eyes gleamed with possibility.

Nobbler's reply put her down a bit. He didn't share her self-centred interest. But then of course he hadn't those three young lasses on his mind. They had to be kept off the streets.

'Aye, but ah couldn't dee that to Stan. Not to Stan, he's me mate.' Nobbler shook his head against that.

Bella sniffed. 'Ah wasn't asking you to do it Stan. But would you do it to Buller?' Bella knew her man.

Would he do it to Buller? That was a different matter. Stan and Buller were poles apart.

'But ah don't run for Buller, so that rules that oot! Besides, how can our Jos carry inside information? He's stuck at his work. He starts at one and doesn't leave till six. Nee time to get ower here with information.' That was the end of the matter. Their flying son was trapped at work, all day.

Bella's glum look told the story. But after all, she was only funnin'. Only theorizing.

A week later she was all smiles. Had she consulted Jinny?

'You or wor Bob start runnin' for one of the big bookies. One of them Newcastle fellas. They can afford a few pund. We'll just give them a short back and sides, like wor Jos does. We'll not cut aal their hair off. Just give them a trim.'

'Ah thought ah'd convinced you there was nowt deein',' Nobbler growled. 'There's nee way aroond that clock and wor Jos doesn't finish till six.'

Bella had that enigmatic look. It developed into a smile, a

grin. 'But wor Jos has every Wednesday off. It's shops half day. He's off at one, every Wednesday.' The grin widened. 'And wor Annie's Billy, he knaas aal aboot clocks. There's nowt he doesn't knaa aboot clocks.'

She sat back in her chair with hands clasped about her middle. She wore her fat-cat smile of satisfaction. She waited for Tom to pick a few holes in her theories.

'We'll only have a win every Wednesday. Once a month. Just give the bookie a trim. He'll never notice.' She could feel that store book in her pocket getting warm.

After all, it wasn't cheatin'. It was usin' inside information, just like the toffs and the nobs.

Things proceeded well. They had a winner every Wednesday, one a month. Of course, not even a brilliant general like Bella could promise a good priced winner every Wednesday, so it did work out at about once a month.

'Let's not get greedy. Just enough to tide us through. We might just make enough before that bugger ower the watter twigs and puts the mockers on. Ah'll get wor Nellie's three settled in sarvice, pray God, before we gets warned off.'

It was Jane Marie Smith who noticed fleet-of-foot Jos Dobson. She took an interest in him, but not for his running ability.

She caught him one Wednesday. It was no accidental meeting. She lived two streets away and stopped him bottom of her street.

'It's Wednesday!' she announced as he arrived panting to impart his weekly information. 'You do short back and sides on Wednesday? Doesn't you?'

Jane Marie liked Jos. He was as trim and neat as she was scruffy. An exhausted Woodbine hung from her pallid lips. She was a picture of imperfection. A landing ground for second-class nits. Her hands and nails in almost perpetual search. She did some searching as she confronted the startled Jos.

'Eh?' was all he could think to say.

'You does short back and sides, Wednesday, doesn't you?'

She had a worried look. The Woodbine collapsed and she searched for another. She was open-mouthed as she waited for an answer. Her breath was the utterance of low tide; it conjured a picture of rotting cats and dogs floating in Woodbine ash.

Jos, gasping for breath after his run from 'ower the watter', got the full benefit of it. He almost swooned.

'Got to go!' he gasped. 'Ma will be waitin'.' He went off like the wind away from that noxious gas. Did Jane Marie know about that inside information? He raced off.

He raced through the lane at the back of his house, through the open back door into the yard then into the scullery. 'Lame Duck at fifteen to one in the first race at Wetherby!' he gasped to the waiting Bella. She got to it with the betting slip.

Jos pumped for breath. 'Hey, that Jane Marie, her in the other street, she stopped me and asked me aboot short back and sides on Wednesday. Do you think she's twigged?'

Bella was shocked. It took time to take in the sense of it. Was that 'dirty bitch' on to them?

They soon found the reason for Jane Marie's waylaying of young Jos. She appeared puffing for breath and of Woodbine at the back door. Her cawing voice carried into the house.

'Mrs. Dobson, Mrs. Dobson, can yor Jos come and shave me Da? Mrs. Dobson, are yer there, Mrs. Dobson?'

Bella's eyes bulged. She looked at Jos as if he was to blame. She scanned the back window.

'The bugger is at the back door! That dirty bitch! Ah'm not havin' her in ma hoose. Go oot and see what she wants.'

That proved unnecessary. Jane Marie was already at the scullery door. She was not to be put off. Bella went to the door to bar her way should she have the affrontery to step across her threshold.

'What you want?' Bella demanded. She stood like the

Rock of Gibralter. A human plug to a gap through which nobody and nothing could pass.

Jane Marie stopped dead at the sight of the district's chief matriarch. The drooping Woodbine drooped further. It was like being faced suddenly by the Queen.

What does a simple-minded person do when suddenly faced with the most influential woman in the district? Jane Marie was too callow to know her place. She would scratch her front or rear with equal abandon in front of the Virgin Mary.

'Ah want yor Jos to give me Da a shave. Ah'm willin' to pay thrupence.' She gave Bella what was supposed to be a sweet smile. She still had all her teeth and her smile was a presentation of a black and brown grid caught with a sauce of baccy and yesterday's chips.

Bella said, 'He's got nee time. He's too busy!' Let her young Jos go into this bitch's hoose? Not likely! She put up a barrier. 'It would cost sixpence, anyway!'

'Thrupence now and thrupence at the end of the week!' It was an honest offer. What could Bella say? Jane Marie was as innocent as only her particular circumstances could make her. Bella relented.

'Aye, alreet! If Jos wants to, mind, it's his time.'

Jos wasn't at all keen on the idea. He was wary of Jane Marie. He'd heard lurid tales about her; all exaggerated. She'd never seen soap. Never taken a bath, not ever! Had strange men in her hoose and, she boozed at the dreaded 'Coffin'. There were other rumours whispered only under the cover of cupped hands.

In fact Jane Marie was merely an unwashed, uneducated, unmade bedfellow. A product of poverty and no guidance. A year with Bella when she was younger and she would have been a far different person. The sight of her strengthened Bella's resolve to keep Nellie's three daughters off the path down which Jane Marie had rolled.

'Ah'll dee it for thrupence! Short back and sides for

thrupence.' Jos showed his good heart. 'Ah'll come roond after ah've had me dinner.' Jane Marie flashed her multi-coloured grin and went off, scratching her rear.

'Mind you put yor cap on, and mind you keep it on when yor there. You never know what you might pick up there. And mind you come straight back!' It was with these instructions ringing in his ears that Jos went off to give that vital service.

He was back in fifteen minutes; white as a sheet!

Bella was livid. What had that dirty bitch done to her lad? 'What she done? What happened, Jos?'

He'd sat down to recover from whatever shock he'd had. Bella began to worry. A virgin lad like her's in that den of nits.

'What happened, wor Jos?' It was as near an endearment as any of her 'bairns' was likely to get. The tender feeling was there, if the words were not.

'Ah went in and she asked me if ah wanted a cup of tea.'

'You said, no, our Jos?' Bella guided.

'Aye, then she asked me if ah wanted a tab ...'

'You said, no, our Jos?'

'Aye, ah said aal ah wanted to do was get the job done and get away. Said ah was goin' out to the pics.'

'Then what did she dee?'

'She said, he's in there, in the front room. So ah went in, and there he was, deed drunk, as stiff as a board. Ah asked her for hot watter to shave the old geezer. After she got the hot watter, ah asked her to take the two bairns oot the room. They was jumpin' up and doon on the bed and ah couldn't shave him proper. Ah might have cut him and made him bleed. Ah did cut the poor chap, but he didn't bleed. He didn't bleed, Ma, because the poor begger was really deed. Ah'd been shavin' a deed man and ah didn't know it, Ma.' The horror of it all still registered. Jos wouldn't sleep easy for some time. It was the first time he'd seen a real deed man.

'Ah, you poor lad.' Bella could have laughed but didn't dare. It was undeniable that Jos had had a shock. Bella on the other hand had seen many a 'deed man'. She'd said, 'Sometimes there's nee difference'. She tried to take his mind off it.

'You was sayin' there was bairns in the room? Bairns, and her not married. There was nee other men there, was there?'

Jos shook his head. 'No, Ma. But ah nearly laughed; ah was tryin' to get away and she said, "Wait hinny and ah'll see if me father has thrupence in his strides". Ah said, 'No ta, missus, it's free. Ah scooted off.' He did have to laugh at it, eventually. Wait till Da and Eddie got in. What a story to tell.

Annie and the Two Vases

'Ah'll send wor Annie aroond to Jane Marie's,' Bella said. 'Ah'll not go roond mesel. That might upset Mary Whitehoose; that's her groond.'

So the major-domo was sent round to do the neighbourly thing. She wasn't pleased. She didn't like Jane Marie so wouldn't enter her house. She stood at the door of Jane Marie's house and transmitted her family's consolation. It was paintful duty to the scruffy unfortunate. Bella's ambassador said her piece and departed. There'd not be much bother in disposing of the old man's estate, two clay pipes and half a packet of shag. Annie handed over the quarter of tea and half a pound of sugar, 'Just to help with the tea, hinny. You'll be needin' it for the funeral.'

Annie could have done with that tea and sugar herself. She too was on hard times. 'Nee harder than others!' she would have said. Billy and her were on the Gardians since the dark days of the slaughtered pigeons. The 'Gardians' didn't actually guard anybody. Recipients of benefit had to prove they'd be a greater burden dead, before receiving a handout to keep them alive; so it was held.

'Ah was thinkin' of sellin' my two good vases.' Annie mentioned this to Annie Summerfield as she made the dust fly from a carpet. Annie – Mrs. Billy – did a bit for Annie the Jewish lady. They got on well together, the two Annies. They were in the same room when little Tombo was born.

'Ah don't like sellin' a weddin' present ... they was from my Aunt Meggie, her who sells flowers outside Grainger Market, but the bairn needs new shoes and my Billy has nee work. If ah has to sell them, how much is they worth?' This was on the consideration that Jews, being keen business people, would have a better idea of true values. Besides, those two fine vases might be antiques and therefore valuable.

'I wouldn't sell a wedding present, Annie.' Annie Summerfield paused to think that over. 'At least, I think I never would. Hang on to them awhile. Little Tommy might get new shoes, somehow.'

'Yor askin' for miracles. They don't happen here. We's Free Church here. We kiss neebody's feet and expect nee miracles.'

'Alright Annie, bring your two vases over and I'll have Mr. Summerfield try to put a value on them. But if I were you, think about it first.'

At the first opportunity, Annie brought her two vases to the Summerfields. Yendall, Annie's husband, was busy rummaging in various boxes. Annie, Mrs. Billy, took that as a sign of a 'business man'. So he was, a jack-of-all-trades, as inquisitive as they come. He viewed the two vases with little or no interest.

Mrs. Billy was crestfallen. It had been a wrench to even lift the vases from her mantelpiece. The theory that they might be valuable enough to separate her from her standards began to fade when Yendall failed to take an immediate interest.

'Leave them with me.' He hardly raised his head.

That put Annie down further. 'Can you tell by the mornin'? If ah leave them with you now, will you know by the mornin'?' She would have swept them up and out of the house if he'd hesitated.

'Alright, Mrs. Billy, I'll see, by tomorrow.' His quick eyes hardly lifted from his rummaging.

Soon as Annie was gone he made for the two vases. He scanned them for particular markings. What did he see in what he saw?

Next day, Mrs. Billy presented herself. Annie Summerfield smiling led her into the living-room. Yendall was, as ever, rummaging in his endless bric-a-brac.

They stood like twins, the two Annies, waiting on a man. He kept them waiting. If Annie Summerfield was used to waiting, Mrs. Billy wasn't. She had great but not endless patience. Was she not Bella's major-domo; a chip off the old block?

'Well?' Mrs. Billy enquired. 'Ah'm here!'

The other Annie quaked at that. Jewish ladies of that time waited until spoken to. She tried to hush Mrs. Billy. She wasn't to be hushed.

'Well, have you made up yor mind?'

There was nothing else for it, Mr. Summerfield had to give them attention. He smiled at Mrs. Billy but not at his wife.

'These are two velly nice vases, Mrs. Billy.'

'Vases? Oh you mean varzzes? Oh aye, they's very nice. They looks nice on my mantelpiece. How much?'

'They are worth fife shillings.' He went back to his rummaging, eyes averted, his ears straining for reaction. How would she take it?

Mrs. Billy was in a quandry. Five shillings would buy those shoes for her bairn. Shoes to keep up with all the other children prettied up for the visit of King George the Fifth and Queen Mary to open the new Tyne Bridge.

What should she do? Mrs. Billy pondered. The image of that grand New Bridge and its Royal patrons loomed large. She looked at the other Annie; she shook her head negatively after a quick glance at her husband. Mrs. Billy looked at her in surprise. She was almost ready to take whatever would buy those new shoes, but, here she was, being given the signal not to sell. Were they worth more? Seven-and-six, perhaps? It was an oscillating time.

The reality of the situation broke through. It was shoes for the bairn she wanted; after all, she expected Yendall to make a bit for his-sel. Mrs. Billy was about to say, 'Alright!' when the other Annie burst out with, 'They are worth more!' She had broken with tradition. She'd gone against her husband.

They could both see Yendall stiffen. Jewish ladies weren't expected to involve themselves. Mrs. Billy guessed her friend would be for it. That silent bond between developed into practicality.

'Is that aal? What a pity. It's not worth the bother, Annie. Thank you for yor time, Mr. Summerfield. Oh, by the way, Annie,' her voice rose as if she wanted more than one person to hear, 'my Big Aunt Mary did catch Big Dan. Aye, she caught him in the Castle; she put the sod in hospital for three weeks. He'll not bash my sister Jane again, ah'll bet. That's the way to treat men that bashes their wives, isn't it, Mr. Summerfield?'

Mrs. Billy gave a sniff and went off with her two varzzes! She gave Annie a smile and a nod. She hoped that Mr. S. would take her kiddin'. She wouldn't want to set Big Aunt Mary on him. It wouldn't be fair, he was only half the size of Big Dan.

They had to meet again, those two Annies. The major-domo had a stern inquisitive look in her eye.

'Everything aal reet, Annie?' Mrs. Billy kept a wary eye and ear for that 'little sharp bugger', Mr. Summerfield.

'Yes Annie, thank you,' came the reply with a smile.

Mrs. Billy gave Annie Summerfield the once-over to see if she had any bruises. 'He didn't clout you, did he?' She wondered what Annie's clothing could hide.

'No, he wouldn't do that. He lashes with his tongue. It can be as painful as a whip at times.' Annie's face saddened at the thought.

'Aye, sticks and stones, Annie love. Ah'll take the tongue any time, so would our Jane.' It had to come. The mystery had to be solved. 'Why did you stop me sellin' my two vases?'

'Why did I stop you?'

'Aye, why did you take that risk with Yendall? Ah know he can be funny, like.'

There came a silence as Annie searched for an explanation.

'Why did I stop you? Well, it is difficult to explain. You see, there's much more to life than money.'

'Aye, that's reet,' agreed the major-domo. 'Sister Winnie keeps tellin' us that.'

'Yes, there are other things in life, much more important things. When I got out of Russia and came here to your country, well, this country is like heaven to me. I know it doesn't seem like that to you; but it is to me.'

'Aye, they do say that Bensham is the Jews' Jerusalem,' the major-domo nodded in agreement.

'Yes, yes, that's right. This is a step to Jerusalem, and speaking of Jerusalem, perhaps that's why I stopped you from selling those two vases. You see, back in the great Solomon's time, when the great Temple was built, there were two tall pillars erected at the entrance. Your two vases reminded me of those two pillars. Two pillars guarding YOU. You are that temple. The pillars in Jerusalem were called, Boaz and Jachin. You could call your two vases, Billy and Tombo!'

The major-domo was amazed and open-mouthed. All she could say was, 'Whey y'bugger!' She'd keep those two special vases. Is that why Bella, her mother, had those two brass candlesticks? The major-domo began to see things differently. Did her mother call her brass candlesticks after Nobbler and her first son, Thomas?

Annie Summerfield smiled at the effect her philosophy had on Mrs. Billy. She'd expected a more practical reason for keeping the vases, but nevertheless was tickled pink with that reason.

'If your two vases had been of Solomon's time, they'd be priceless, but in a way, sitting on your mantelpiece, they are still priceless.' Mrs. Billy continued to beam at Annie's edifying knowledge.

The Great Goalie!

With no money from the sale of those now hallowed vases, other means had to be found to buy those new shoes. Not that Tombo didn't have shoes. Shoes he had but he lived in a district where foota was a religion. A religion practiced every day.

Out of the clouds the 'tip' came. You could get shoes, well, beuts, if you were on the Gardians. It also wasn't all that easy. Maybe Sister Winnie had something to do with it. Maybe Annie Summerfield?

Yes, young Tombo got boots. But what was that man doing punching three holes in them? Spoiling them according to Tombo.

Those three punched holes could hardly be seen by an onlooker. They were there as identification in case the claimant tried to sell them. But Tombo the wearer, he could feel or imagined he could feel those three holes in the form of a triangle. He'd try anything to lay off wearing them.

'The other lads is runnin' around in their bare feet,' he piped that day, that glorious day. The day the great bridge was to open. He wanted to get rid of those new boots. Those three holes were a mark of distinction he had no desire to own.

When those boots came, young Tombo, as stubborn as his parents, viewed those boots as a let-down to his plan. He had piped, 'Get a piece of paper from Gran.' A 'ticket' from Miss Mulligan?

'Them pieces of paper have to be paid for!' the major-domo had retorted, but smilingly. While the little fella sat on the fender observing comings and goings he thought it all an exciting game. Those bits of paper were magic and that Miss Mulligan was such an elegant lady.

And now here he was, all togged up with his new boots, new short trousers and new blue blazer with its brass buttons. You needed more than new boots to be fit to meet a King. He was now as near the King as he'd ever be.

The street and all other streets were ablaze with interest. Jos, Uncle Jos to Tombo, was prominent with his double-breasted waistcoat. He didn't have boots with three holes in. He had natty shoes with a fashionable point. Real toff's shoes. It was such a burden to bear to see the other lads and his cousins running about in bare feet and Uncle Jos beside him with the poshest of shoes. Tombo tried to hide his embarrassment behind his well-brushed hair-peak, thick enough to be an eye-shade; if only that hair-peak was long enough to cover those three holes.

Tombo was certain that his cousins and the other lads regarded him an outcast. How could he know that those without shoes envied him? But those three holes still bored into his feet showing his mark of charity.

Aunt Jane's lads had no shoes. That didn't seem to bother them. They could climb lampposts and drain-pipes with equal ease in their bare feet. Tough as teak they were. As adventurous as mountaineers; and as with mountaineers, no pinnacle was safe from exploration. They would be chased with cries of, 'What you doin' up there, you fool, have you got nowt better to dee?' 'Just gettin' the baal!' would be the eternal cry in return. Recovering the lost ball was a never-ending exercise for the bare feet brigade.

The day was fine and sunny for the visit of the King and Queen; dare it be otherwise? The major-domo's lad had new shoes. Two very important factors to ensure good weather.

There was the New Bridge spanning the Tyne, sparkling new in its bright paint, reflecting the bright sun. A soul-stirring work of art. This special day would be a fair excuse for a booze-up. Bella had already put her order in for an extra jug of best bitter at the Blue Light. 'Just in case, hinny.' Everybody seemed happy that day, all but one. He had boots with three holes in.

'Yor gonna wear them boots whether you wants to or not!' The major-domo had said it most firmly. 'What does it matter if they's three holes in them? Sit on that step and keep outa mischief.'

Sister Winnie came on the scene, making her rounds of the streets nearest the Mission. She came smiling as ever. Nodding to this one and that one, her taffeta tail-scarf fluttering in the breeze. Well scrubbed and dainty, she was feared more than Big Aunt Mary; it was a different sort of fear. She might persuade you that you were less than good if you did not attend Sunday School. You had to have your star-card full of stars if you wanted to go on the annual trip to South Shields.

Strong men's knees had been known to turn to jelly under her charismatic persuasion. Local long-time drunks could be seen carrying her banner on Saturday night. Saturday night was battle night; the battle against demon drink.

All this was in the name of a fella called Jesus. She broadcast this every day.

She stopped at Bella's house to pay her respects to the group gathered at the step. She smiled as only she could smile. Nobody had ever seen her without that smile. She went to bed with that smile, so it was said.

Some children gathered. Others escaped, too bashful to face such a grand lady. Her impediment was her well-washed appearance which made others feel inferior. She talked funny too.

'Well then, Thomas, it is Thomas, isn't it?' She had a posher voice than Annie Summerfield. She beamed at Tombo like a lighthouse seeking lost ships. 'He's a shy little fellow. What's the matter, little boy?' Had she guessed about those holes?

The major-domo whispered in Sister Winnie's ear. She responded with an ever-widening smile and focused on Tombo. He shrank back out of the sunlight. He would have liked to have fled back in the house to the safety of Gran and Granda, if he dared. The major-domo however was determined to have him in the front line.

Sister Winnie clapped her hands in unmistaken joy, as if she'd made an earth-shaking discovery.

'Do you know that it was Doubting Thomas who didn't believe? Yes, it was Jesus too who had three holes in his, er, sandals.' She looked at Tombo, the great rebel, the modern-day doubter. He glowed red and dropped that hair-peak further to hide behind. Sister Winnie had her theme and she plugged it for all she was worth.

'Yes, children, it was Jesus himself who had those three holes in his hands and feet. He is our Saviour! God bless all who carry the same marks.' She led them all in song, beating time with her hands. 'Jesus loves me, that I know ...'

They were all soon engrossed in singing, and Sister Winnie moved on bowing and smiling to all on that fine June day. No doubt she would make someone else's day with a further sermon.

When he was sure that inspired gleam of hope had moved further up the street, Tombo dared to peep out. He was dying to ask who that fella Jesus was, but wouldn't dare ask that beautiful lady.

Whoever that fella was, that funny woman thought he was great. But why should she think him so important? Was he the new goalie for the Magpies? She'd said he was a saver. Uncle Jos and Uncle Eddie had said that the Magpies would be the greatest team in the world, if they had a better goalie ...

But this fella Jesus, he also had three holes in his beuts. That made two fellas with three holes in their beuts. Tombo didn't feel quite so much in the spotlight now. But was Jesus as good as Hughie. Hughie Gallagher as far as he knew, didn't have three holes in his beuts ... Bet that fella Jesus wasn't as good as the great Hughie Gallagher ...

PART FOUR

Abdication

It appeared to be established that Hughie Gallagher did not have three holes punched in his foota beuts.

Tombo had suspected it. His uncles, brought into the plot, had assured him Hughie did have three holes in those magic beuts. Beuts that encased those educated feet. Those three holes were part of the magic.

Would his uncles take him over the watter to see the great Hughie standing in those beuts with three holes? That proved to be an exercise without possibility. His uncles lost some of their particular magic when they couldn't produce the goods.

Tombo confirmed his allegiance with Doubting Thomas by piping, 'Ah'm not wearin' them beuts till you shows Hughie's beuts with three holes in!' And he meant it. Head down, thumb in mouth, other little fist clenched.

'That's showin' them, Tombo,' Nobbler exclaimed with a grin. 'You tell 'em, son. They'll have you believin' in Santa Claus next.' Nobbler chortled at Tombo's spirit.

'Hold yor tongue, you!' Bella snorted. 'Yor spoilin' the bairn's dreams. You get them beuts on, you little tinker. Beuts doesn't grow on trees, and get that thumb outa yor mouth.'

Even the stern matriarch couldn't move him. Only sons could be treated like little princes. When you were in that singular position and didn't have to share anything, beuts with three holes in weren't fit for princes, if they wanted it that way.

As for that other fella, that Jesus fella, him with them three holes in his sandals, according to Sister Winnie he was only a goalie. Goalies weren't even as good as wingers, never mind centre-forwards, like Hughie Gallagher.

He thought they were all daft. He didn't say so because he was a 'man' of few words. When things were 'daft', when he suspected, by some magic inherent process, that elders were giving him blarney, he'd adapt that pose of head down, left hand clenched and thumb in mouth. Try and shift him.

He was now sure that the great Hughie did not have three holes in his foota beuts. Yet another step forward out of babyhood.

He'd sent out his, 'I don't believe you' signal when he was at infant school. They'd wanted him to wear that silly hat with the elastic band and pretend to be a mouse scampering across the floor. Prancing around while the teacher plonked away on the piano. He'd thought that quite silly. Foota was much better.

He'd sent out his signal of protest. They didn't understand; said he was stubborn. He was, but not daft. That prancing around, it was for girls and children.

He took another step forward when he noticed, when all others did not, that ducks had webbed feet. Teacher thought he was marvellous. He was no longer stubborn, he was observant. He'd been trying to tell everybody that for years.

He was immediately promoted to the back row of the class. A singular honour. All the clever pupils sat at the back. The dunces sat at the front under the teacher's eye and reach.

Without knowing it, he'd taken part in a streaming exercise. His teacher had first thought him gauche. She wasn't so sure now. Tombo thought she was silly to make such a fuss over so small a matter; everybody could see that ducks had webbed feet. How else could they propel themselves through the water in Saltwell Park lake?

Nevertheless it was good being in the back row. No marauder from the Askew road gang could thump you in the back. On the other hand, you were last out of the classroom. That marauder could wait for you. If you were a clever boy, you could have enemies.

It was about that time he stopped putting his thumb in his mouth. The major-domo had gone to some length to train him away from that. Why didn't she know he was merely thinking? Various recommended concoctions, evil-tasting, were applied to that precious thinking organ. None worked. Whatever was put on it was licked off. Nothing can stop a thinker from thinking.

'Little tinker seems to like aal we put on,' Bella grumbled. She knew aal about bairns, but not this one.

It was Nobbler, his Granda, who cured Tombo's thumb sucking.

He was sitting in his usual place, polishing his pants on the fender. His cousin Isabella, thin and bony and older by one year, had the affrontery to take his place. The Place he'd polished for years. She soon was elbowed out. She could sit on the other side; she was a girl.

Bella shooed her away. 'Yor not sittin' there lass! Yor too near the fire. Did ah tell you what happened to her upstairs? She fell asleep with the poker in the fire. It fell oot when it was reed hot and set the place alight. She was deed by the time yor Granda got tee her. You stay back from that fire.' That seasoned finger pointed Isabella back to Tombo's side.

Isabella slid back along to that privileged side. After all, she had a perfect right, she was a princess.

The prince, he didn't fight with girls. They were beneath him. He rose, reluctantly, to put his mind to other things.

This gave him a chance to study the workings of the opening and closing of the oven door. Exploration was better than fightin' girls for a seat on the fender.

The clanking of exploration began to interfere with the gossip. It was fascinating, that lever that lifted and clanked, and locked the door of the oven.

Bella looked over in exasperation. Her glare had no effect on the explorer.

'Can't hear mesel speak! Make that tinker stop that noise, Tom. Little tinker is always playin' with that oven door.'

Nobbler rose to obey. To save his granddaugher having her head bashed in by that swinging iron door. He took the shortest route and shut the iron door, on that famous thumb.

If Tombo never sucked that thumb again he also looked at his Granda in a new light. He'd be sharper now; you couldn't even trust your own Granda now. As for sittin' on that fender, that was for lasses. He had better things to do.

With the thoughts of those beuts and that jambed thumb looming largely, it took a visit to Aunt Annie's to bring new adventures to wipe out those former disappointments.

Aunt Annie wasn't Tombo's aunt, she was the major-domo's aunt. Grandma Bella's sister.

Aunt Annie had eleven children. Even Tombo's eyebrows popped at that. But he'd been once before and he hadn't seen eleven bairns all in one room. It was exciting, all the way up those flight of stairs.

His Ma didn't think it exciting. She was on a duty visit; an ambassador for Bella. She didn't mind the visit but the thought of, 'carrying aal that watter to carry up aal them stairs to wash aal them bairns.' It didn't bear thinking about. 'Y'see Tombo, there's always somebody worse off than yor-sel.'

Did Aunt Annie have three holes in her shoes? That was his greeting. That was going to be his greeting. The major-domo was getting tired of the same old questions so he held fire. But, did Aunt Annie's children have holes, three holes that is, in their shoes. It had to come out. He'd feel better if somebody somewhere had those three holes in their shoes.

'Have my bairns got three holes in their shoes? ... What's he on aboot, Annie?' The major-domo told her.

Aunt Annie was a lightweight carbon copy of her sister Bella. She laughed at Tombo's serious question. The major-domo shook her head in exasperation.

'Aye, aye, ah suppose they has holes in their shoes. Them that's got shoes. You's a very lucky lad to have new shoes.'

Oh, was he? He didn't feel lucky. He moved to the window to reflect. Again he was on a short rein.

'Don't go too close to that winda! It's a long drop from there.' You couldn't escape that eagle eye. Not for a second.

He knew it was a long way down. That was the interesting thing. That's why he'd come, to look out of that window.

Aunt Annie's flat was perched high over the Tyne. You could see Newcastle quay; the hot-chestnut man. His little oven fire glowed in the dark. Tombo could almost smell those hot chestnuts and roast potatoes.

It was Sunday night and what he liked most were the bells from St. Nick's and St. Mary's. St. Nick's in front of him sounding from over the Tyne and St. Mary's at his back. He thought they were marvellous. Some of the other residents in that block of flats didn't share his enthusiasm.

That was the trouble with mothers. You could never get to lean right out of that window and see what was going on below. Of course there were times, when she was busy gossiping, you could lean right out and see those ant-like people below. He wondered if he could hit one of them with spit. He only wondered about it; never did it. He'd get a clout if the major-domo caught him. He knew he'd have to aim before the people were directly below him. If only he dare.

He asked where the 'back' was. He wanted to go.

Aunt Mary said. 'The netty's doon-stairs son. Gan doon to the bottom. It's in the yard.'

The netty's doon-stairs? That was a new one. That's what they called the 'back'. Why did they call it that?

He went down all those stairs to the yard, to find this place called the netty. Was it a sort of net? He knew what a net was. That's what he caught the tiddlers in at Saltwell Park lake.

He was on the bottom floor when he took a wrong turning and found himself in a candle-lit room. There was a man in there, and he was doing something with his hand. Tombo had to stop and look.

He was an old man, gnarled with age, and if not beaten down by the weather of his experiences, they had left an indelible mark. He made Tombo's Granda look like a youngin'. Tombo just knew that this was the oldest man he had ever seen and as such he had to receive more than passing scrutiny. It was later he discovered this was Aunt Annie's father.

The old man turned and gave him a toothless grin. He nodded but got on with his work. Work lit by the light of four candles reflected by old mirrors.

'Aye, aal he does now is paint.' Aunt Annie had that to say about her father.

'Paint?' asked the major-domo. 'How much does he charge? Ma would like our house painted.'

Aunt Annie had laughed at that. That would be a useful pastime. It was laughable if you wanted to laugh about it. Aunt Annie couldn't afford to laugh. Not with eleven children, a wayward husband and her rather odd father.

'He's not a full shillin'. Aal he does is paint. If he painted waals that might be handy, like. But he just paints ships and boats and bords. He's real daft now. Gets old ships' sails and hangs them on the waals like waalpaper.'

'Paints on old ships' sails? Like waalpaper? Ah thought he was a fisherman? Ah thought he salted fish in his room?'

'Aye he still does that. He's got little bords in little crees on the waals as weel.' Aunt Annie frowned. 'He's a bit micey now.' She leaned forward to whisper. 'Got to watch the lasses. As ah said, he's not a full shillin'.'

The prince was already in the presence of he who wasn't a full shillin'.

'It's a duck!' Tombo pointed to the image on the large canvas hanging, nailed, on the wall.

It was clear that the old man was unused to such interest in his work. Not by such a connoisseur as a back-row expert. He stood back in surprise and this sudden movement caused the four candles to flutter and throw wild shadows about the room. It was hardly possible to paint by candle-light but the old man appeared to be succeeding.

'Hrrm!' The old man cleared his throat. Or was it a grunt of displeasure? He was painting for pleasure. Now he had a critic. He turned back to his work and ignored his critic.

There was no reward in identifying that duck. With his new-found weapon for making friends, or enemies, his unique observation, Tombo thought he'd made a friend. After all, this man might not know what a duck looked like. He tried again.

'It's a duck!' Tombo pointed with friendly determination.

There was another bout of throat clearing. An off-red handkerchief was wielded to a venerable proboscis. Without turning, the old man growled.

'It's a goose! A goosey-gander.' The goosey-gander bit to match the age of the critic.

'It's a duck! It's got skin on its toes!' came the reply, accompanied by that imperial pointing finger.

The painter turned to confront his critic. The old against the young. One looking up, the other looking down.

'It's a goose, a goosey-gander.' Was it a question now?

The imperial head shook in disagreement. That finger stabbed again.

'It's a duck.'

The old man turned to re-examine his handiwork. The little birds in their cages on the wall seemed to flutter as if awaiting the outcome.

'Naa, it's a goose. It's supposed to be a goose, son.'

'It's got skin on its toes! It's a duck!' That piping voice was insistent.

'Gooses has got webbed feet as weel as ducks.' The old eyes gleamed in triumph.

That was a new one. He thought they had skin. But the old man called that, webbed? You learned something every day. Did goosey-ganders have skin on their toes as well as ducks? He stepped forward for a closer look.

'It's a duck! It has a snout like Barney's.' That clinched it as far as Tombo was concerned. Barney had a boozer's nose. A snout like a duck. Skin on its toes, and a snout like Barney – it must be a duck. The glorious duck that had promoted him.

Caught picking his nose, Tombo was informed by the major-domo, 'You'll get a nose like that Barney Haze, a nose like a duck.'

The old man's nose got an extra good clearing out. His eyes watered at the pressure and the feathers flying among the watchers in the shadows.

'Well aal be buggered! Aye, well lad, ah's not changin' the bugger. It'll be the only Barney-billed goose in the world. It's faather musta been playin' away!'

Cold Rice Pistol

Tombo liked Barney Haze. He was jolly and a bachelor. He was often tipsy. He did foolish things when he was 'on the beer'.

Barney's greatest asset, as far as Tombo was concerned,

was the enormous pistol he kept in his drawer. The major-domo did a bit of cleaning for Barney's sister and Tombo often accompanied her.

Barney's nose and Barney's pistol occupied a special place in Tombo's mind. Barney's nose was classic. In addition to being large and red it was pitted with prominent deep purple holes. That nose and that pistol, brought back from the war, set Barney apart from others.

'Will it go bang, Barney?' Tombo had asked when allowed to handle that pistol.

'Naa son, it's not that sorta pistol. It's what they calls a Very pistol. It shoots greet big lights. It's for seein' Garmins in the dark.'

It took both hands to steady that big pistol. Tombo dreamed of shooting those dreaded Garmins. He would have taken that pistol home if Barney had agreed. Barney did not agree.

'What does Garmins look like?' Tombo aimed the pistol at every one of Mrs. Haze's ornaments, standing in as Garmins.

'What does Garmins look like? Ee, ah don't know, Tombo. Ah niver saw any. Ah expect they looks just like them pork butchers, next door to the Reedheugh.'

Tombo did know them pork butchers. They were healthy looking and clean. Their shop was spotless. They couldn't be Garmins. Barney was pulling his leg.

'Aye, they's big and fat is yor Garmins. Aye, just like them next door to the Reedheugh. That comes from eatin' too much pork. Yor Jews is thin and yor Garmins is fat. The Jews eats nee pork, that's why they's thin. You never did see a fat Jew, did'ya?'

That was true. Tombo had never seen a fat Jew. But then, he hadn't seen more than Annie Summerfield. So, Garmins is fat and Jews is thin; he'd remember that next time he saw a Jew or a Garmin.

Tombo had digested all this information while eating his

cold rice pudding. Barney's sister kept it for him from Sunday. Should the major-domo do the cleaning on Monday, the rice pudding was sweet. Tombo wouldn't consider it on Tuesday. The pudding could keep him partly occupied on Monday, if that was cleaning day. Should cleaning day be Tuesday, that drawer with that pistol would receive attention. If Barney was in bed asleep, being a night-shift worker, Tombo would urge the major-domo to wake him. Barney was best off the scene as far as the major-domo was concerned.

'That pistol is between you and yor wits. Yor like a bairn with its rattle.' She'd sneak it out of Barney's drawer nevertheless.

Tombo the bairn would take that soldier's rattle and proceed to shoot at all that looked like a fat Garmin. He was extra careful not to shoot at the many crucifixes and Virgin Marys that adorned the house. Mrs. Rice was an ardent Catholic.

So it was that other people's dwellings became an association of sights and smells. Barney's red nose and his Very pistol and Mr. and Mrs. Rice Barney's sister and brother-in-law.

While Barney was preceded by his outstanding proboscis, Mr. Rice was preceded by the odour of 'best bitter'. He was a very smelly interesting chap, quiet and friendly.

Mrs. Rice was always most discreet about the best bitter. Her journey from the Blue Light with the jug was made incognito by virtue of hiding that jug under her apron. The Virgin was too much of a lady to look under your apron.

If Barney's house was an association of Very pistol, large red nose, cold rice pudding, and crucifixes tinged with slight odour of best bitter, Aunt Annie's house was important because of its location. There you were king of the castle. No Garmin could cross from Newcastle when you were standing there with Barney's pistol, not even at night. Six storeys up you could see everything. It's a pity Barney didn't understand. You could have a great time with that pistol, up there, waitin' for them fat Garmins. But then, on the other hand, if you wanted a wee, you had to travel all the way doon them stairs, at night?

He was glad that he'd bumped into that old chap, that old gadgy. He was a bit backward, still, old people were like that. He didn't know the difference between a duck and a goose. Just look at Barney, he didn't know how important that pistol was; always hiding it away in his drawer. He'd even locked it now!

Come to think on it, you did meet some strange folk at these other places. Granted Aunt Annie's place had great interest because you could watch out for them fat Garmins from that high winder. Walter didn't believe him and he'd offered to prove it. The major-domo wasn't too keen on takin' Walter. She said something about, 'One tinker bein' enough to cope with.'

But you did meet strange people there. There was that big lass. She wanted to help him take his trousers down. He didn't care to have that done to him. Why did girls always want to take his trousers down? Walter had said it was their eternal instinct, or was it, maternal? Walter didn't know what he was talking about. Only the major-domo was allowed to take his trousers down. But lasses were funny.

Take Isabella for instance. She wanted his seat on the fender. She'd got it. He wasn't interested any more. Besides, he wasn't too keen on his Granda now.

He'd found Isabella in his bed. He didn't know till next morning. It always took him a long time to wake and it was some time before he realised he wasn't alone. He was annoyed and footed that strange lump out of HIS bed. Everybody had laughed but it was no laughing matter.

In this large family you had to be prepared to receive others in your bed if married couples fell out and had a fight. The bairns were grabbed by the major-domo on the instructions of Bella.

'Fight it out among yor-sels. You'll not get the bairn back till you's do!' That was how you could wake up next morning and find a strange lady in your bed.

Fading Dreams

Very pistols and cold rice pudding and further dreams of guarding the town against the Garmins were replaced by more mature dreams of foota and cricket. Dreams of playing for the school team.

Walter, a year older than Tombo, had a great scheme. It was called, knocky-nine-door. Tombo wasn't too keen on it.

'Why do you call it knocky-nine-door?' he asked.

'Whey man, it's caaled knocky-nine-door because you pick on every ninth door, do'ya see? You ties a lang piece of black threed, black threed mind, oot yor Ma's sowin' box, and then you tie one end to number nine's door-knocker.'

'Why every ninth door?' enquired Tombo.

'Cause nine is the sign of the Divel!' Walter chortled.

Tombo digested that. He didn't believe it. He said so.

'But there's only one Divel.'

'Aye, that's reet. But them that lives every ninth hoose, they's the Divel's disciples.' Walter grinned at his cleverness.

'Garn, it was Jesus who had had disciples.' Tombo knew that cause Sister Winnie had said so.

'Aye well, that's what they say, them that invented this game. But Tombo, if you play knocky-nine-door, you mek sure it's through the week, and niver on Sunday.'

'Why?' Tombo asked.

'Because the gadgies are oot till five. It's safer when the

gadgies are oot. If they come oot stead of the wives, they'll chase you till they catch you and belt yor arse.' Walter grimaced, maybe from experience. 'Knocky-nine-door can be chancy if the gadgies are in the hoose.'

Tombo decided that knocky-nine-door wasn't as good as foota or cricket.

Apparently the rules for knocky-nine-door were capable of wide interpretation. All the houses in the block where Walter lived got a bit of black threed on their door-knocker, eventually.

Cricket got an airing every summer. They'd be playing foota every day then suddenly, it would be too hot for foota. Then the stumps would be sought.

Tombo's school had a set of stumps. They were collapsible and needed no bails. Bails or not, those who craved for cricket played on. The best footballers didn't shine at cricket; it was too slow, so they claimed. They played foota all the year round.

Only a tennis ball was allowed in the school yard. The genuine 'corker' was banned to the playing fields. It was there the pukker cricketers used that heavy hard ball. Those who they said had met Jack Hobbs. Bowler Strong was one of those who had met Jack Hobbs, so he claimed.

Bowler had a set of stumps with bails. He also had a real cricket bat.

A real cricket bat could take the force of that hard ball. Home-made cricket bats shielded the user from the force of that heavy hard ball like a lightning conductor is shielded from lightning. You'd be jarred to your toes if you did owt more than stone-wall. Bowler could win all day.

Tombo and the others didn't mind. They were interested only in the game. They guarded their wicket with enthusiasm if nothing else.

There was never a full team, just enough to bowl and field for the great Bowler. Bowler was also the umpire. He was the only authority on the rules of cricket. It was worse than having the only ball, the only backyard, and the only rain-barrel, in the hands of a hostile.

The group consisted usually of Farta Jones, Wellie Loughlin, Sparra (ankles) Casey, Bowler, and Tombo. They were all well named.

Bowler did have bow-legs. He was no good as a goalkeeper for that reason. For the same reason he was no good anywhere on a football pitch. Hence his love of cricket. Cricket he felt was his forte. He knew the rules backwards. The others were certain those rules tended to favour a certain bow-legged fellow. But they never bothered to study the rules, so they couldn't complain.

Wellie Loughlin always played football in his wellies. No one could remember seeing him without those wellies. They in no way impeded him. They had the double advantage at cricket where they served as protective pads. Shin guards at football and shin guards for cricket. Wellie had great verve on the foota pitch and the cricket pitch. A little too much for the great Bowler who feared the wiry Wellie.

August was the time for cricket. They had four weeks holiday. Four weeks to do as they liked. If you expressed only the very slightest interest in cricket, Bowler was your immediate friend. A constant bowler to the world's greatest batsman, apart from Jack Hobbs.

The craze could last three weeks if the summer was good. They'd play all day in the rain at foota. But somehow, they hadn't the same dedication for that other game.

The lads didn't believe Bowler was the world's best cricketer. They were ready to believe he was the world's greatest actor. Of that they had no doubt. There was a theory that the real reason for these cricketing sessions was not to witness Bowler's cricketing prowess, but to see somebody funnier than Charlie Chaplin.

No cricket pads were worn. Only cissies wore pads, in the truth of the matter, they couldn't afford them, not even Bowler. If they had the misfortune to stop that hard ball with a bare knee they were permitted to hiss with the pain. Even a sharp yell was permitted. Then they got on with it. Bowler would continually offer advice on how to take guard. After all, he had seen Jack Hobbs play.

Bowler always took longest to take guard. He would pat down every bump on their make-shift pitch. He never fielded. He bowled, he batted, but the running after the ball, that was for the learners.

Wellie had the wellies. He was the one to plodge into the 'Gut' if Bowler managed a good clout. A hit into the Gut was a sixer, Bowler would be delighted. Wellie would not be, but he was the only one with wellies.

If it came to a diving job, four pairs of eyes would settle on Farta. That combined effort would persuade him it was his job. In he would go with encouraging shouts that he was the best swimmer. Remarks about, 'You cud dee with a bath, Farta!' did nothing for his feelings.

The craze could end as quickly as it began. Only the going down of the sun would bring that game to an end; then on the next day, if the weather was good, they'd be at it again.

They'd sweat and strain to serve the master. Their right arm would have grown two inches and be as stiff as a cricket stump. The only cure for bowlers was more bowling.

It was Bowler's antics that finally took the edge off the craze. They could stand his antics while they thirsted for the sound of that click of ball on bat. When that thirst was quenched they no longer needed to bend their knee to that paragon of cricketing virtue. Their tolerance level dwindled as the summer wore on.

It was Bowler's umpteenth performance of the summer that finally ended the craze. Down he went when a ball from Tombo caught him on the knee. He rolled over and over in great agony.

'Sorry, Bowler!' Tombo gasped, 'Er, leg before wicket?' He offered that apologetically.

The antics stopped immediately. Bowler lay on the ground then sat up. 'What? Whey no, man. You was a mile out!' He immediately went again into writhing agony. The others gathered around. They'd seen it all before. This was once too many.

'Where does it hurt?' Tombo asked, sympathetically.

'It's me knee, it's me knee! Ah think it's broken.'

'Garn!' Farta blurted. 'You's a better actor than Charlie Chaplin.'

Tombo held up his hand. He felt responsible and he could send that ball down with some pace, but with enough to break a leg? That was doubtful.

'If it's his knee, we should get some cold watter. Cold watter to reduce the swellin'. Let's have a look, Bowler?'

Bowler wasn't having any. No amateur was going to doctor him. He rolled around, still in the greatest agony.

'You could get some cold watter in yor wellie,' Tombo suggested to fielder Wellie Loughlin.

Wellie didn't think much of that. He had a better idea and gave it.

'There's plenty cold watter in the Gut.' He looked gleefully at the others. 'Let Charlie Chaplin cool off in there?'

No sooner said than done. They picked up the world's second best cricketer and carried him to the waiting cold water bath. In he went with a splash. They had to carry him in so they too had a bath.

In cricketing terms that was what became known as an early bath. It was the great Bowler who invented the term because it happened to him. Actually, he knew the lads were paying him homage because of his prowess on the field.

Growing Higher Dreaming

Tombo was the youngest in the group that always seemed to stick together. Lads from the same street or near. He'd become monitor in all his classes at school. He'd had an easy time at school; lessons were no struggle to him. On a number of occasions he found himself 'put up'. Elevated to a higher class. If this was a mark of progress, it had the disadvantage of putting him against older boys.

He who was only two or three months older than Tombo could be handled. When he came up against lads a year older, he had to take a back seat. Chosen as chief monitor by Mr. Haigh, when he was not the oldest boy in the school caused a bit of a stir. At only thirteen he was now the 'milkman'. It was his job to collect the daily milk money and see to the distribution of milk. Lessons for him were coming to an end.

His counterpart in the girls school, on the floor below, was a well developed young lady. A foot higher than Tombo. It was rumoured heavily that she had two tennis balls stuffed down her jumper.

'Tennis baals?' Farta had exploded. 'They's more like case-baals!' More mysteriously, 'Ah saw her with a man last neet. She was sparkin' in the lasses passage.'

A man in the lasses passage? That was a sensation. A lass from their school, seen with a man. A big fella?

The boys were segregated from the girls at Tombo's school. Separated by high walls and tall spiked railings. If you were thin enough, you could squeeze through those railings; it wasn't done, but if you felt adventurous, it was far better to wait till Miss Morrison was not on playtime duty. If she got her eagle eye on you her squawk of protest would bring out the fire-brigade.

The chief fireman had a big stick and was called Mr. Waite. That big stick could put out any fire. The headmaster was fire-chief.

You could get that big stick for any number of reasons. Coming in late. Talking while in line. Talking back to your teacher after he had whacked you with his cane. If you farted in class you were sent out into the school yard to be aired. Farta was the chief offender, hence his title. Caught smoking in some secret corner, you wouldn't think of smoking again till the pain of that big stick on your rear end wore off. That could take weeks.

It got to Miss Morrison. That a man had been seen with that big lass. He was the milkman. Off duty of course ... attracted by them case-baals. He wouldn't return, not after that wigging.

They were beginning to notice things. Yes, when you lifted yor head from the foota, it was true, lasses did have tennis balls stuffed down their jumpers. Why did they do that?

It was Walter who knew the truth. He had sisters.

'They's not tennis baals. They's more like big plums and they's not reed. Lasses hasn't got taps like we has. They's got nee taps so they canna scoot up waals. They's got to sit when they has a wee, ah've seen them.'

Walter had seen them? He was the sensation of that day.

But there were other sensations. Things perhaps of a more important nature.

It was at the 'Tin Hut' at Dunston that Tombo became transfixed. Hypnotized by the voice of a great singer. The silent cinema had gone out and was replaced by the all-talking, all-dancing picture.

When your musical education had been restricted to the sound of the piano played by Peggy Benn and singing Rule Britannia on Empire Day, you could be forgiven for acting like a village yokel when struck by the mighty voice of Nelson Eddy, singing in Rose Marie.

It was true he enjoyed evenings around the piano, singing, or trying to sing, to Peggy's playing. It was true he liked the singing at the 'Mission' run by the indomitable Sister Winnie, but this fella Nelson Eddy, he was a real God. Nelson Eddy was the world's best man. Hughie Gallagher and his Uncle Bob and Uncle John, considered to be pretty special, paled to insignificance when compared to this new phenomenon.

That the human voice could emit such wonderful noises came as a tremendous shock. It was an absolute miracle.

Tombo was in a daze for weeks after hearing that mellifluous baritone. Yes this was truly the most remarkable man in the whole world. A man who put even Uncle Jos and Uncle Eddy in the shade. Even Johnnie Gray, his father's best friend, who used to give him money, even he wasn't as good as Nelson Eddy. There was only one better than Nelson Eddy, that was his father, Billy, husband of the major-domo.

Of course, his Dad Billy, he had bought an old boat. A ship's lifeboat. He'd brought it all the way from Sunderland, by sea. That journey alone in that little boat made Tombo's Dad all the more outstanding. Yes, even better than Nelson Eddy.

He didn't get down to the garden as much now. He had that other hideaway, beneath the big shed where Freddie Gray kept his motorbike. He used to guard the place from Garmins.

The garden was one of many on the sloping banks of the river. The main path between individual plots was a cinder path, refuse from the nearby gas-works. The boundry walls consisted of anything that came free. Lots of garden walls still had the stink of gas about them being constructed of old gas-filter frames. Tombo never found that smell offensive.

When much younger, he'd offered to stay all night in that space under Freddie's shed; just to make sure the Garmins didn't attack. He'd invited Walter and he was keen too. His Dad and Johnnie they weren't too keen. The major-domo wouldn't hear of it.

They'd had it all planned out. They'd roll those sleepers and other things lying around to make a barricade. They could watch from behind that. The spiders were a nuisance; both he and Walter didn't like spiders. But then, there was that blowlamp in the shed, they could use that to fight off them spiders. They guarded the place all day and didn't see one Garmin. They'd even guarded the place without the blowlamp, suffering them spiders.

It was a problem of elevation. Freddie had said so. They were facing the right way, but weren't high enough. Aunt Annie's house was high enough, but underneath the shed, crouched behind that barricade, they could just see over that flower-bed filled with dahlias. Couldn't even see the Tyne.

The major-domo was right, as usual. Even though as back-up they had Johnnie's big dog, Prince. He was keen too, they could tell. But on second thoughts, Prince was a bit too keen on the sandwiches and he didn't seem to understand you had to keep your head down. He kept running off to bark at anybody who had the nerve to walk along that cinder path.

The major-domo was right. 'The little tinkers will be back soon as they gets hungry!' How would she know that?

It was that big dog, Prince. He ate all the sandwiches. Dogs are nee good for watchin' for them Garmins. All they can dee is bark and keep you awake.

It was boats and engines now. They were off to Sunderland to buy an engine for the now converted lifeboat.

Boats, messing about in boats, could be hard work. It was also lots of fun. What was it about boats, no matter how old, no matter what the shape, that drew like a magnet. At least they drew Tombo like a magnet.

Not far from the Tin Hut, where he'd been introduced to

the great Nelson Eddy, and in Dunston, was Devlin's boatyard. There Tombo's Da kept their boat.

It was high and dry most of the time. Only the spring tide was high enough to float the boats that used Devlin's as a winter mooring. Just the place for fitting out. It was a case of do-it-yourself. None of the fellas who kept boats there wore gold braid on their caps.

Converting ships' lifeboats was a time-consuming exercise. A good therapy if you were unemployed, as Tombo's Da was. He was good with tools and had gutted the lifeboat and created a nice cockpit and cabin. Hence that journey to Sunderland for the engine.

They decided on a Bedford petrol engine. Big enough to propel their now twenty-four foot cabin cruiser.

Getting that engine was one thing. Understanding it was another. However, all problems are there to be solved. With the help of other boat men they soon understood about engine bearers and propshafts and prop sizes and prop pitches. Straight through gear-boxes were yet another problem.

Tombo's Dad did most of the work. His partner in the cabin cruiser was Johnnie Gray. He left most of the wood and mechanical work to Billy. Johnnie was a foreman in the local glassworks. A very important man. Very kind to Tombo.

So here he was again, beside the Gut. The River Team, a tributary running into the Tyne.

This was the same Gut the lads had thrown Bowler in. The same, yet not the same. At Devlin's they weren't far from where the Gut fed into the Tyne. Here, the water of the Gut at Devlin's was black and oily. Back up river, where they played cricket, a mile away in open green fields, the water was muddy but clean.

The water at Devlin's was an industrial sewer.

Still, where there's muck there's money. So it was said.

On the opposite bank was the local iron and steel works,

the buildings themselves far back from the river. Somebody in some authority had decided to dump, for whatever reason, drums of solidified redlead. Perhaps they'd hardened beyond use. The Gut was the dumping place for all not wanted things.

Redlead was just the thing for undercoating for boats. Most of the boats at Devlin's had their bottoms undercoated with a mixture of well-worked boiled oil and redlead. Industrial fall-out had its uses. Do-it-yourself crumbs from the rich man's table.

Tombo still remembered that ground on the other side of the river. It was where the gang played on their way back home from the Saturday matinee at the famous Tin Hut. Walter would look out for the 'gadgy' – the watchman. If he wasn't in sight, they'd sneak onto that ground with its heaps of interesting paraphernalia.

They'd play, regardless of time, in those interesting and strange steel boxes stacked outside the foundry. They became impregnable fortresses against the Indians or the Garmins.

If they were extra daring they'd climb the handles on those metal boxes, right to the top. When you got there, you could risk dropping inside. Inside, right out of sight. Shut off from the outside world. It could be funny though, if you couldn't get back out again, the major-domo would be worried. Worried, and mad at him.

There were little holes in those moulding boxes. You could watch out through those holes for the gadgy, or Indians or Garmins.

The major-domo always knew where Tombo had been on Saturday. If he had a bloodshot eye, he'd been, 'in them damn boxes again.'

If he had tar on his hands, the gang had dallied on those two gas pipes that ran parallel with the little bridge across the Gut near the Gas Yard. Crossing the bridge was for cissies. The gang crossed the bridge on those two pipes;

after all, if them Garmins bombed the bridge, the only way across would be by them pipes. Those pipes were covered with pitch to protect them from the weather. Nobody ever discovered anything to protect those pipes from small boys.

Butter was the only thing to take tar off your hands. Grandma Bella used to measure the butter. One teaspoon for rubbing tar off hands.

There was no real risk. If you fell off the pipes into the Gut, the water underneath was only two foot deep, at low tide. They weren't daft, they only crossed at low tide. You couldn't drown in two foot of water if you fell off those pipes, but, by the time you got back up top again, you'd be covered from head to foot with sticky black slime.

It would take more than a teaspoon of butter to bring you back to normal.

And there were all them diamonds. That place where them metal boxes were stacked was littered with diamonds. Diamonds of all colours. That was the real reason that gadgy was on guard.

Nobody would believe them. But if them diamonds weren't diamonds, why where they stored in them metal boxes? They were as strong as any bank safe.

The glassworks where Johnnie worked was next to the steelworks. Tombo asked Johnnie. He would know, he was a foreman. Johnnie confided that them diamonds was real diamonds.

'Aye, they's diamonds alreet, Tombo. But they's rejects. Not good enough to gan oot. We only sends oot the gooduns'.'

The lasses called them diamonds, 'boodies'. Lasses didn't know much!

While the growing Tombo could now look over the Gut from Devlin's landing to that diamond field, he could chuckle at the memory of those former days.

That little bridge with the big gas pipes had been

superseded by a fine new white bridge. There were no tramcars now to bump and sway over that little bridge. There it was, looking like a miniature alongside its new big brother still surrounded by those youthful dreams. No longer would they have to face up to ambush from those Askew Road Apaches. No longer would they have ride on the bumper bar of that Dunston tram to hide from that imaginary flight of arrows.

Greater, more realistic dangers were now on the horizon.

PART FIVE

God's Watter!

They had a year of it. Boating on the Tyne. They went up stream to Ryton Willows. It was a hot day and Johnnie bought them all a bottle of lemonade. A whole bottle of lemonade for Tombo; he could hardly believe it. Johnnie was a generous fella.

They went downstream to the sea. Tombo felt distinctly queer when they went over the bar. He was sick, to his great shame, till somebody told him, 'Nowt to worry about, Tombo. Even Nelson was seasick.' That did help a bit. If that fella had said Nelson Eddy was also sick, that would have been even better.

Before they got over the bar, that cruise downstream had been quite nice. Sitting there watching the rolling wake with that steady beat of that engine, had an almost therapeutic effect. It was he who had gone for the petrol. He'd carried that two-gallon can a whole mile from Kyle Road. The only petrol pump in the district. Or was that the only place you could buy Power petrol? That was why the boat was cruising so well, it was that Power petrol he'd carried. That bumping against his shins had been worth while.

They'd had to put ballast in the boat to bring the stern down. That had been a problem, the stern was too high meaning the propeller hadn't enough bite on the water. It was alright now. But a success to some people merely pointed the way to further experiment.

Tombo's Dad had a brilliant idea.

'We'll put a counter stern on her, Tombo. What say?'

So it was decided. The boat would, when the summer was over, be put back on the hard at Devlin's and have the old stern taken out and that new counter stern put in. Their boat would no longer look like a converted lifeboat.

It was at this time that Tombo began to learn how to bend wood. To bend the new ash ribs for that adventurous counter stern which would put more room in the boat.

The first attempts to bend those ribs ended in failure.

To bend ash ribs to the shape desired needed a steam-chest. You had to 'cook' the wood and when hot enough, bend it to the boards of the clinker-built boat.

Where could they acquire a steam-chest? That required observation. Tombo's Da was an expert on reconnaissance. As he had said, 'Time spent on reconnaissance is never wasted.'

Tombo was and remained impressed at the number of things boatmen can acquire for their hobby.

For their steam-chest, Tombo's Da produced a drain-pipe. With a wooden bung in one end the ash rib, well pre-soaked, was introduced into the drain-pipe. The free end was choked with an old rag after a gallon of water was poured into the pipe.

A small fire provided the heat, the fuel for the fire being in abundance about the boatyard. They manoeuvred the pipe over the fire in such manner as to heat the pipe just above the wooden bung. The pressure emitting from the end partly choked by the rag gave them indication of the softening process.

It was a hot job and a disappointing one. The hot ash rib was hurriedly clamped to the gunwhale and then with boot and young and not so young strength, the rib was forced into the correct curve.

The very first rib ruptured on the most acute part of the curve. When the second attempt was also a failure they rested their hot hands and red faces. It was a time for thinking it out. What was wrong?'

'Ah think it might be the watter, Da!' Tombo almost put his thinking thumb in his mouth. Perhaps it was the clash of that oven door, deep in his mind, stopped him.

'The watter? What do ya mean lad?' Billy, Tombo's Da, took another draw on that Woodbine that magically appeared when they had a rest. He could work all day without food, but not without a Woodbine.

Tombo had asked his Da some time ago, 'Why do you smoke Woodbines, Da?' He'd heard that Woodbines were made from materials very unpleasant. Why didn't his Da smoke Capstans? The best cigarettes.

'Why do ah smoke Woodbines?' That blue smoke drifted along the roof of that little cabin. 'Because they's cheap, ah suppose.'

'Ma doesn't think they's cheap!' It came out as it would come out of an innocent.

Billy didn't like that much. It sounded as if somebody had been discussing him. He said nothing to Tombo; he couldn't understand. So he thought.

'Aye, she thinks they's too dear,' Tombo rambled on, not knowing how he hurt.

'She'd think them a hell-of-a-lot dearer if they was Capstans ah smoked!' Da snapped back. There'd be words when he got home.

'But why does men smoke?' That inquisitive mind didn't stop. But he wasn't talking just about his Da. That made some difference.

'Women smokes as weel,' Billy countered.

'Ah know, but why does anybody smoke, Da? Sister Winnie says, "If God wanted folks to smoke, he would have put a chimney on their heads".'

Billy leaned back against the cabin sides, enjoying that

Woodbine. He didn't give an immediate reply.

'Aye, she says only chimneys are meant to smoke,' Tombo continued his theme with a grin.

'Aye, aye!' Billy did enjoy a smoke. 'Aye, maybe she's right. She's good woman.' He took that Woodbine out of his mouth and tapped off the ash. 'Aye, next time you see Sister Winnie, Tombo, you tell her from me, when you's buried yor pals just yesterday, and it's rainin' like hell, when yor usin' their graves as a backrest and an arm or a leg pops out at ya outa the mud and God's gone on holiday, maybe a fella can be excused a Woodbine or two, to settle his nerves a bit. You tell that to Sister Winnie, Tombo.'

So that was why Tombo's Da had started to smoke Woodbines. Only eighteen and living cheek by jowl with his dead companions. Out there in France, fightin' them Garmins in the muck and blood of battle. It was the first time he'd spoken about the war. Yes, his Da was better than Nelson Eddy.

It was some years later that he discovered his Da had a receipt for twenty-three Garmin prisoners. Yes, Nelson Eddy had taken a back seat. He couldn't be seen in the presence of a man who had captured twenty-three Garmins, single-handed of course.

The cost of Woodbines was never raised again in the major-domo's household.

Billy drew on that now respectable Woodbine. He would never be without one if the awe-stricken Tombo had his way.

'You think it might be the watter, eh Tombo?' They understood each other better now.

'Aye, you wouldn't put that Gut watter on yor dahlias would you? You wouldn't put that watter on yor tomato plants, would you?' Tombo awaited an answer from that now real hero.

His Da nodded his head, not in agreement but in thought. He was never one for rushing things. He nodded his way through his thoughts.

'Aye, rainwatter is alreet for the gardens, and it's full of little bugs.'

'But that Gut watter, it's got a lot more than them little bugs. There's a mixture of deed cats and dogs. And there's oil and coal tar, aye and that reedlead.'

'And Woodbine dumps?' Billy's eyes gleamed in merriment. 'Aye, and it's still sweeter than the watter at Ypres, and there's nee poison gas here. Ah know, ah got a touch of that gas.'

Would there be no end to the adventures his Da had had? Tombo grew three inches that day. But he was as tough as the major-domo and his Da.

'Ah still think it's the watter! If we canna drink that watter cause it would poison us, maybe it will poison that wood?'

That beautiful Woodbine was again sucked for inspiration. 'Umm, when the watter boils in that pipe, shouldn't that kill off aal the bugs?' Da wasn't as simple as some youngins' might think.

It put Tombo down. It was true. His teacher had said it. If you boil watter, it will be fit to drink. If it wasn't the Gut watter, what could be the reason for the ruptured ribs?

'Bad batch of wood, eh?' Da offered a way out.

'Aye Da, might be, but ah still think it's the watter.'

So, it must be the watter. Tombo had said so.

'We need good clean watter to make a good clean bend. The better the watter, the better the job!' He was adamant, was Tombo.

The Woodbine was out now. Exhausted, but it had refreshed the smoker. He made extra sure it was extinguished by stubbing it on the cabin floor. He then trod on it. It was time to go to work.

'Aye, tell you what we'll dee, lad, we'll gan back home and get some dinner. On the way back we'll caal at St. Joan's. We'll take a gallon can and get oursels some watter oot the font. If it's good watter you want for them ribs, let's get the very best. The priest blesses the bugger every day. Nowt but the best for this boat, eh, what say, lad?' He winked at Tombo as he gathered up the tools.

Tombo wasn't sure if his Da was serious or not. After all, a man who had fought with and captured twenty-three Garmins, buried his mates in mud and had been gassed, and had done all that for a packet of Woodbines, he might be a man capable of pinching a gallon of God's watter.

They proceeded with tool bags on shoulders from the boatyard to the new white bridge spanning the Gut. Billy stopped and looked over the parapet. Only five foot two inches, he could just see over the top.

'Aye, it's true about holy watter. It does wesh yor sins away, just like this Gut watter. That's why folks chucks aal the things they don't want inta the Gut. They's tryin' to wesh their sins away.'

Nothing that the hero of Ypres said would ever be questioned by Tombo.

They walked together over the bridge and came to the Gas Yard bank. It led to St. Joan's at the top. They passed the place where that man with the hand-pump would pump out that funny watter. Gas-loaded watter. Watter that would burn like paraffin so Walter had said.

'Does this place, the Gas Yard, does it smell like that gas, out there at that place in France?' It was asked hesitatingly. It was now not easy to speak to a real hero.

His hero was silent all the way to the top of the bank. It was when they came level with St. Joan's that he spoke.

'It's not the same gas, lad. The gas from the Gas Yard is for lightin' hoozes. That Garmin gas, that was for puttin' yor light oot!' He pointed over to St. Joan's. 'There's yor good watter. Aye, and speakin' of watter for bendin' ribs, Gods musta used the best watter when he made yor Ma.' He sighed, not a thing he did. 'To marry a fella like me, nee job, nee prospects, and now, Woodbines is too dear to buy.'

Tombo could have burst out with, 'It must have been the

best rib to start with!' But that was the sort of thing you said later, when you should have said it sooner.

They walked up Rose Street to their branching-off street. Billy said, 'Say nowt to yor Ma!'

Sacrifice

Maybe it was the clean tap water, or maybe as Da had said the ash had been wrongly cut against the grain. Whatever, all the ribs were bent into shape without problem.

It was hard but rewarding work. They pressed on and they were at the painting stage. They might get her off the hard at the next high tide.

They called the boat Shaun Gray. The name-boards were made and painted. They never did get screwed to the bows. Johnnie Gray died suddenly.

That sudden death knocked them down. A fella like Johnny, dead! It was hardly believable.

After a decent interval, the question had to be asked. Johnnie wasn't married but he had brothers. Billy asked Freddie, he who had the motorbike shed; under which them Garmins were watched.

Billy was told, 'It's yours, Bill. You did the work?' It was true, Billy had done most of the work. He always did.

Johnnie never did crave to be a boating man. Not like Tombo. He could live with boats all day.

They had their boat but the garden was now gone. Gone to make way for the building of council houses. Their loss would be somebody's gain. No more cabbages, no more pretty flowers for the major-domo. None of those huge tomatoes would grace the table. Life was, except for the freedom given by the boat, closing in on them.

Petrol cost money that they could ill-afford but they still

pottered about in that sweet little cruiser that brought admiring glances. Converted lifeboats with individual counter-sterns weren't thick on the ground.

Tombo could remember that day well. It was a day when he could feel excitement in the air. He could feel it as soon as he entered the house. His Da was talking to the major-domo.

'Aye, there'll be a job for Tombo as well. Mr. Timpson says he can get Tombo a job as an apprentice at Wickers.'

A job? An apprentice at Wickers? That was all the young fellows dreamed about. A permanent job. A steady job at that famous factory.

Tombo already had a job. Quite a good job. Not as far up the ladder as being an apprentice at Wickers, but a good job by the standards of the time.

He left school and had tramped around looking for work as was the custom of the time.

Somebody offered him work pushing a barrow around the district. Taking ordered goods to customers. That was not the job for him. He tried for only one day.

'Everybody has to start at the bottom,' the major-domo had snorted. If the thumb didn't go into the mouth any more, there were other ways of showing his inherent stubborn streak. Tombo made it plain that a travelling barrow-boy was not his forte. Not a job for a fellow whose Da was a hero.

It was Uncle Eddy's friend, Susie, who got him out of that fix. She spoke for him and he got a job at Wilkinsons' soft drinks factory. He would be a delivery boy. A mate to the driver of a pop lorry. It carried more milk than pop. He thought that strange.

Now he was a motorized delivery boy. More his style, he knew about engines. This was far better than pushing a barrow.

His job, after the initial training, was to work the load. Keep the full crates of Dymo milk at the lorry's edge so the driver wasn't kept waiting. Wilkinson's ran a clean smooth image. All transport had to be kept sparkling clean. All vehicles were washed every night without fail. Mr. Harry and Mr. John, the owners, were mobile managers always on the job.

Tombo's driver was Jack Bristoe, a most genial man. He grew to like Jack, a fair-minded man.

They carried the milk and an assortment of pop. They'd line up in their turn at the loading chute. Everybody worked. As quick as the crates came off the chute they would stack them for safe travel to Sunderland. That was their stamping ground.

If they had to wait a few minutes, Tombo would nip in to see Susie at the bottling plant. He was surprised to see how much dirt could be taken out of fresh milk. He now knew how to test for fresh milk without opening a bottle. Just by tapping the bottle in the right place.

They travelled to Sunderland every day. Tombo got to know all the roads to Sunderland and its outlying districts. Sometimes they called at the great Vaux brewery to pick up crates of beer. He thought that was most odd. A milk lorry carrying beer. What would Sister Winnie say about that?

They were days of warmth and tranquillity for Tombo. He became familiar with the sights and smells of Sunderland. A place of warmth, in his opinion.

And there was the money. He'd never had so much money. He had all of twelve shillings a week. Twelve shillings and sixpence a week! Two to three shillings a week as pocket money. Rich living indeed.

He was about to leave that rich living behind.

He became an apprentice at Wickers. That great armaments factory on Scotswood Road, Newcastle upon Tyne, over the watter. That is to say, he would become an apprentice when he reached the age of sixteen. He was not yet sixteen.

He reported to Wickers that special morning. He had to

find Fred. Not Fred of the motorbike shed, brother of Johnnie, but Fred the foreman millwright; another boat man. A very handy man to know.

Finding Fred was a problem. He had a little office tucked away among great thundering machines. Tombo felt lost in this world of whirring, clanking, whizzing noises. He found Fred at last and he was taken into the safety of that little office out of the menace of those noisy giants.

Fred inspected the new man. All five feet of him. Tombo wasn't tall but he was well filled.

'So you want to be a moulder, eh Tombo?' Fred was a quiet man; he had a bit of a limp. A moulder? What was that, Tombo thought. He didn't say anything. He could almost hear the major-domo say, 'Be a good lad on yor first day.'

Fred walked around Tombo, clad in his new dark-blue overalls. He gravely bent down to that new back pocket and pulled away the label that said, 'Sale Price' four shillings. The major-domo had forgot to remove it.

'Right lad, ah'll take you to see Col. He's the foundry foreman. He'll show you what to dee. The foundry is doon the road a bit. Got yor bait? Right, well leave it here with yor new tea-can. Come back here at bait time and ah'll mek some tea for us, seein' it's yor first day.'

That was how Tombo met the great Col, the head foreman in the foundry. A commanding figure even among foundry men. The mystique of foundry work was such that even the Managing Director, whoever he was, would never challenge the great Col.

'If you can dee it better yorsel, dee it!' That was a statement of fact that brought all argument to an end. Col knew those chairbound critics couldn't dee it.

Fred introduced Tombo to Col the foreman. Tombo didn't realize the importance of Col. He was just a man in a white coat with a fanny hat.

The two foremen exchanged a few words and Fred went off to his duties, after reminding Tombo about bait time.

'Come with me, lad!' Col waved Tombo along the foundry floor. He led the way among the moulders working on their individual moulds.

Tombo thought he detected a slight note of resentment in Col's voice. He certainly didn't treat Tombo like Fred did. But then, Fred was Da's mate and Col wasn't of the boating fraternity.

'This is young Billy, Billy, this is Danny. He'll be yor mate. Danny'll show you what to dee. Take yor coat off and hang it ower there.' He indicated a big nail offering its services.

Danny was a quick, dark-eyed lad, taller than Tombo and older. They grinned a greeting.

'Yor name's Billy, eh?' he asked Tombo.

'No, my name's Tom. My Da's name is Billy. Ah don't know why that man called me Billy. Billy's me Da's name.'

'Righto then, Bill, this is what we dee.'

Tombo did get it across to them eventually that his name really was Tom. Named after his Granda; him who had cured his thumb-sucking.

Tombo, now Tom, got another surprise. When you were an apprentice, you were expected to work for next to nowt. You got the privilege and, seven shillings and sixpence a week. A week, lying on. You did a week's work and got paid the next week. His pocket money was down to a shilling a week.

But now Da was working and working overtime. He got four pounds a week. Four pounds a week? It was unbelievable.

He spent all morning with Dan, watching closely what moulding was all about, If it hadn't been so interesting, he might have thought, 'This is nee place for a fella whose Da is a hero.'

The foundry was a dirty mucky place, yet full of mystery. Complete strangers came up and gave him advice. 'What's yor name? Are you in the Union? Get outa here, son! What made you want to be a moulder? Ah couldn't get my lad in. Who do you knaa?'

'Tek nee notice, son!' It was Freddie Jordan who worked in the same corner. 'Just tek yor time and you'll dee alreet. Aye, and divint be a tear-arse like that Danny. He doesn't knaa when to stop. Always leave some work to dee for tomorra.'

Came bait time, twelve o'clock, and he tried to re-trace his steps back to Fred's office. It was Monday and Fred had large thin slices of fruit cake; he gave one to Tom. Good backing for cold fried egg sandwiches. That insistent hooter beckoned all back to their toil and off he went, back to his mate, Danny. He who was a tear-arse? What was that?

He was quite prepared to continue to watch Danny that afternoon. Col had a different idea. Tom found that his tutelage was over.

'Hereyar, Bill, ah want you to mek this job this afternoon. Just tek yor time and ask Dan if you get stuck.'

So Tom made his first real job in a foundry. It was known as a half-bearing. An iron casting with eight little pockets. Two put together formed a clamp for two shafts. Shafts that provided power for the hundreds of whirling wheels throughout the works. From that day he never stopped making things.

It was in the afternoon that the real excitement began. It was when the molten iron came streaming out of the furnace to be caught in ladles. First into large ladles and then into much smaller ladles called shanks. The sparks flew like a firework. It was an exciting time until he got a tiny spark down the back of his neck. It burned like a red-hot needle and yet it was only a pin-prick. He tried not to jump about like a jack-in-the-box. The others only grinned.

'Turn yor shirt collar up, lad!' was all the advice he got.

It came time to cast Tom's first job. Freddy and his mate carried that glowing shank to his mould. That flowing-glowing-living liquid was fascinating. It was an excitement that happened every day. Every day that hypnotic glare demanded attention. Every day it demanded and got the great respect it needed lest its glissade should turn to a holocaust.

He came to understand why the furnace was the centre of attraction. The foundry was like a white-hot soup kitchen. Every man getting his share of soup he didn't dare spill.

It could be likened to waiting for judgement. The judgement of the searing liquid. That which would search out any mistake made by an erring moulder.

The next day was the same as the first. Danny was first on the job; he couldn't wait to discover the result of yesterday's work. Danny was a fearful worrier. He never made mistakes. Never made the mistake of allowing Col to see his mistakes. He had his own inspection system. He was his own worst critic. Tom was just as keen that first day to see how that first mould had fared. He cautiously parted his moulding boxes to inspect the result of the cast. All he saw was a heap of ugly black steaming sand. It didn't look promising.

'Yu canna tell till yu gits the sand off. Scrape the hard sand off. Git right doon to the castin'.' Danny came over to offer advice. He was looking pleased so Tom presumed he'd a good cast.

Doing as instructed he scraped away the sand, cautiously.

'Here let me!' Danny came forward with a scraping tool. He attacked the heap with great gusto. Freddie and his mate came to watch. How could anything of any value come from that sorry pile; so thought Tom.

Freddie read his thoughts and grinned at Tom.

'They's like bairns. They's just like bairns when they's first born. Bairns look a right mess when they's born, y'knaa? They look a lot better after the midwife cleans them up. That'll look aal reet when yu cleans it up.'

And so it did. Tom's first casting did look all right when

it was cleaned up. Col came over and had a look. He gave a slight nod of approval. Tom was in.

He'd have liked to have taken that first casting home. True it was a bit heavy to cart all the way back along Scotswood Road and then over the Redheugh Bridge. He was persuaded that the Managing Director himself was waiting to use that very casting. He reluctantly watched it being taken off to the machine shop.

'My Da works here, as well as yor Da, Bill, ah mean Tom.' A huge grin surmounted Dan's face. He was feeling good. No bad'uns that day. He would be cheerful for the rest of the day.

'That's him up there.' Dan pointed upwardly to a gantry high above and at the level of the cupola loading-mouth. He waved to a man leaning over the rail.

'This is the new lad, Bill, ah mean Tom!' he shouted up to his Da. 'His Da works at Wickers tee!'

The man's face widened in a smile and he waved back.

'We'll gan up later and have a look at the furnace,' Dan said. 'How did you get in, Tom? Did yor Da get you in? My Da got me in.'

How did he get in? Into this place of highest standards?

'My Da knaas Mister Timpson!' He just mentioned it. Was he name-dropping?

Dan's eyes widened in interest. 'Yor Da knaas Mister Timpson?' His mouth formed, 'Oh.' He thought that out. How could he best that?

'Ma uncle works here tee! That's him ower there!' He pointed beyond a sort of fence, a barrier of patterns and moulding boxes, which separated their small casting-bay from a storage area.

Tom turned where Dan indicated to see yet another man wave to them. He had his shirt sleeves rolled high to expose huge biceps. As Farta would have put it, 'Muscles big as case baals.'

The man waved them over. Dan looked around to see if 'Snow-white' was about. 'Snow-white' was Col and the other foreman who wore white coats. 'Ice-cream men' was another scornful title. Col and the other foreman were not in sight.

Dan inclined his head in the direction of his uncle.

'Let's away ower there, Tom?'

Tom followed his new mate. His only guide here. Only link with his own age. They sauntered over to what Tom guessed was a forbidden area in working hours.

'This is young Bill, ah mean Tom!' Dan introduced him and corrected himself. He'd get the name right in time.

'Oh aye!' The powerful man grinned at Tom. 'Yor ganna be a moulder, like Dan here?' He flexed those great muscles.

'Can we break some pig?' Dan pleaded.

'Garn!' His uncle laughed. 'You's not strong enough. Little lads like you. Come back next year. You'll get a big baal if you tries to break pig.'

Get a big baal? Tom wondered what that meant. But Dan was anxious to do it. Would he get a prize, a big baal, a case-baal? Tom wouldn't have minded a new footbaal.

He guessed that the lumps of iron lying around were called pigs and that this man was employed to break them into smaller pieces. Pieces that Dan's Da would then feed into that great furnace. It would be worth trying though. He was sure he could earn that big new baal.

He viewed the set-up. The man was tossing the big bit of iron at a huge circular anvil. It looked easy enough, if you didn't have to do it all day. 'Ah can dee that! Ah bet ah can break pig!' He'd said it now. Committed himself. Dan looked crestfallen. He'd wanted to best Tom. He might know Mister Timpson but his Da and his uncle, the strongest man in the place who could break pig all day; that was at least as great as knowing Mister Timpson. But here this new lad was offering to break pig on his very first week. Still wet behind the ears but willing to risk a big baal breaking pig.

'Ah'm first! Yor just a new lad.' Dan jumped in first. His uncle grinned. It was an old trick: get the new lads to fight over who should break pig.

'Only three each! Nee more than three each. Best oot of three, that's how we'll judge it.' Dan's uncle made the rules. He stood back as they limbered up.

The audience were the tall stacks of pig. They looked in silence as the contestants spat on their hands in preparation.

If you were strong enough, strong enough to lift the double pigs chest height, it really was easy to break those pigs into two pieces.

Dan was older than Tom. A couple of inches taller and not an inch of fat. Tough as they come. He knew he could break those pigs. He was certainly strong enough.

He took up a double pig. Staggering slightly at the weight he plunged forward to the anvil. Up went the pig, high as he could get it; down it came with a wallop, unbroken. He said, 'Bugger!'

Never mind, he'd break the next one. He dismissed the first one as a fluke. He'd make sure of the next. He'd give that one an extra wallop.

Up went the next pig, more confidently than the first; he now had the weight. He charged with even great speed at the anvil. His uncle pushed Tom aside as Dan charged; he missed the anvil completely and the pig skidded off onto the pathway. Dan collapsed on the floor. He was up again, not yet defeated.

His uncle waves his hand. 'Git a blaa son, git a blaa. Let young Tom have a go.' Dan was all for having yet another go. He stood back as ordered.

Tom bent down to pick up a pig. They were heavier than they looked. There was no way he could bring it to chest height. He knew there was a catch to it. Strong as Dan's uncle was, even if he had muscles as big as case-baals, he couldn't break pig all day. Not the way Dan was trying to do it.

He rolled the pig over and over, playing for time. Trying to find a good hand-hold. Now he had it. Up it came, to thigh height; he walked to the anvil and finding the exact centre, dropped it a mere ten inches. The pig broke with a sharp crack. The two bits fell one each side of the anvil.

Tom walked back to the stack and did the same with an other two double pigs; it really was easy, when you knew how. Just the same he wouldn't have like to break pig all day. The skin was already scored at his finger tips. Still, Dan's uncle did wear gloves, he'd need to.

Dan was up in arms. 'That's not fair! Yor supposed to throw them. Any bugger can dee that!'

The man with case-baals for muscles was the referee. He'd made the rules.

'Aye, Tom larns faster than you, Dan. You was supposed to break them. Tom's the winner. His brains is in his heed, not in his arse.'

That ended the matter. Dad didn't speak to Tom all that next day. They worked side by side but did not speak. Tom was sorry he'd won the contest. He'd won the contest but might have lost a friend.

But there were other ways of proving you were as good as anybody else, even if they did know Mister Timpson.

He was beginning to hear rough mature masculine conversation. Not the sort of things he was used to hearing. Things he knew were wrong. The wrong side of man. What would Sister Winnie say if she heard some of the things said in foundries? Tom was not to know the things that disturbed him were not the prerogative of foundry men. But of life in general.

Some men he found to be most offensive by their vulgarity. Others he found to be just the opposite. Allan Philips was one such moulder.

Allan was the foundry philosopher. He was a healthy-looking red-faced man. Jovial, always on the go. Tom could never remember seeing him sit down. He was both quiet and loudly complaining. He was a royal. A royal who had earned respect. Mister Timpson would seek Allan's advice on most practical matters. As it appeared that Tom had been touched by Mister Timpson's brush, he was acceptable to Allan's philosophy.

Tom thought Allan had a face like a benevolent teddy bear. He was slightly stooped possibly because of his constantly bending over moulds.

For some reason he always wore red bib-type overalls. These with his ruddy face gave him a warm appearance. A warm man, with an ever welcome smile. A mischievous smile. He always had a little joke. He was an artist in sand. He would place messages in strategic places; jocular messages carved out of lumps of loam aimed at some miscreant who wasn't playing fair. The likeness to the miscreant would be so lifelike there'd be no doubt for whom the message was intended.

To Tom he never ceased to give advice. Allan was on a higher plane than other moulders. Tom was a good listener. He'd sooner listen to Allan than any other.

'What's this for, Allan?' Tom asked him one day. It was some time after those first few mysterious days of introduction to this new skill.

'What's this for? These is balance weights. These is for them new four-and-a-half-inch guns. At least they will be, when they's full a lead.' Allan never stopped working.

'Filled full of lead?' Tom gazed open-mouthed at the four-foot moulding boxes. Boxes that dwarfed his fifteen-inch boxes to nothingness. 'They'll be mighty heavy, lead's heavy, ain't it?'

'Aye, that's the point. They's got to be heavy. Anti-aircraft guns has to hev lots of elevation. They got to balance that lang barrel.'

'Can ah see them guns, Allan?' Tom's eyes gleamed. 'Do you think there's gonna be a war?' Guns and war, they were exciting days for apprentices.

'Aye, could be. Let's hope not, laddie. Still, that's what keeps us workin'.'

'Will we be fightin' the Garmins again?'

'Who else? There's neebody else worth fightin'. Still, not to worry, you'll not be gannin'.'

If that was supposed to please Tom, it didn't. Why would he not be chosen to go to war? Was he not good enough? He had to know.

'Why will ah not be gannin' if there's a war?'

Allan was still as usual pottering about. Tom had to shift himself as the great man moved about his work.

'Why will you not be gannin'? Yor not tall enough for a start. And yor not old enough.'

'Ah might be when the war starts. When will this war start? Ah can break three pigs straight off the belt.' He really was as good as anybody. 'Ah'll be six-foot when ahm twenty-one.'

'No you'll not. How tall is yor Ma?'

'Me Ma? She's as tall as me.'

'Then when yor twenty-one, you'll be a couple of inches taller than yor Ma and yor Da. You'll niver be six-foot. Course, you might be if you put horse-muck in yor beuts. Nowt like horse-muck for mekin' things grow.' Allan was a great gardener. He knew the value of nature's manure. He waved his thumb, 'Shift yor-sel, here comes Col!' Tom sidled off to his own corner. There to think on those wise words.

When opportunity arose, he was back next day. Apprentices were like old-fashioned fags in a college. They 'fagged' for this moulder or that moulder. Dan was the fish-and-chip-man. He'd get out of work before the proper time, 'Ah's got to get to the fish shop before a queue forms,' was his usual excuse.

Tom would have fagged for Allan, only Allan didn't smoke or want bars of chocolate or fish-and-chips, or any of the other things that men appeared to need to keep them going at their work. Allan depended on nobody. But Tom could at least pretend Allan wanted something if the demon Col happened to be about.

He wanted the conversation to be about that war that was on the horizon, and why couldn't he be six-foot high when he was twenty-one? You never get what you want. He got more advice on another subject. One in which he had no interest.

'You'll be gettin' yor-sel a lass?' As usual he never stopped moving about. He was slapping clay-wash on his moulding tackle and Tom dodged smartly to avoid being covered.

'Whey no!' He blushed at the thought.

'Aye, that's what they aal say. Wait till she gets you in the back row at the flicks. You'll not knaa what's hit you.'

Tom didn't want to talk about lasses or back row seats. When will this new war start, was what he was interested in.

'Aye, take ma tip. If you does get a lass, get one that's plain. Divn't get one of them fancy bits.' Allan pressed on with his theme for that day.

There was nothing for it but to listen. Tom put his foot up on the moulding box only to take it down hastily as the great philosopher moved around.

'Aye lad, before you marries her, give her a good test. Tek her to the park and sit her doon on a bench.'

'Ah aint gonna get married!' Tom was scandalized.

'Aye, tek her to the park and sit her doon and tell her to stay there. If she's still there next mornin', she's the one for you.'

'Ahm not gonna get married! What if it rains?' He supposed that would prevent a fair test.

'Aal the better! If she's still there after it rains, she's

either an idiot, or she thinks the sun shines oot yor bot.'

Tom tried to manoeuvre him on to that other subject. The one about being six-foot and that new war with the Garmins. There was nothing doing, not yet.

'If you ever get a pony, tell you what to dee.' It was amazing the way he moved around while giving his advice. 'Niver let its mane or its tail git too lang. Do you know why?'

Tom shook his head negatively.

'If you lets its tail git too làng you'll find its got nee rump. Ponies with lang manes always has poor hindquarters.'

That wasn't as interesting as being six-foot and fightin' the Garmins.

'Aye y'see, the oats you feeds her gans straight to her tail and her mane. Yor feedin' her for nowt.' He moved closer. 'It's the same with lasses.' He was whispering now. 'Them with lang hair has nee bot.' He slapped his own rear-end to emphasize his point.

Tom grinned at that. Maybe he was interested in girls after all.

That teddy bear-like nose poked at Tom in merriment.

'You tek notice, Tom. Just you look at them lasses, see if ahm not right. Them with short hair will have decent bums. You got to have a lass with a decent bum, keeps you warm in the winter.'

So that was how it was? That was worth knowing. Tom was about to ask if Missus Philips had a decent bum but decided he'd better not. It was, after all, a very personal matter.

But they were making progress. Things were moving around to that special subject.

'That's why you'll niver get much higher than you are.' Allan's eyes twinkled. He lòoked benignly at Tom. 'Yor hair's too lang.'

There was the truth staring him in the face. If he cut his hair short and put horse-muck in his beuts, he might grow to six-foot. But what about that war?

'What about the war? How do you know there's gonna be a war?' He had to know and this man was bound to know.

'How do ah knaa there's gonna be a war? Well, they's tekin' apprentices on, aint they? When they takes on new lads there's gonna be a war.'

'How can you tell? What's new lads got to dee with a war?' The questions would never cease.

The great man stopped at last. He was being serious now. Tom could sense it.

'Because two things are needed in a war. There's them that meks the guns, like us. And there's them that shoots 'em. Any daft fella can shoot 'em; it teks brains and skill to make 'em.' He put his foot up on the moulding box, a thing he hardly ever did. 'When they put young fellas in as apprentices, they's choosen' them that's not gonna git shot. War or nee war, yor here for six years at least. It's six years for you, melad, not six-foot!'

That was shattering news. The war was going to miss him and Dan and all the rest of the lads. Tom hurried off to tell the bad news. He turned it all over in his mind as he went back to Dan ... Lasses with lang hair had nee bots, if yor lass was still on the bench when it rained she was a goodin', they were all here to get shot, or, were they all here to stop gettin' shot? It was all good stuff but very puzzling. He wondered if Dan had got that new bar of chocolate?

It was some time later when he discovered the truth. Discovered why a job at seven-and-sixpence a week was better than a job at twelve shillings and sixpence a week. It was a truth that descended like a cloak of kindness.

Maybe he was an apprentice at Wickers, but what a price to pay. Seven-and-sixpence down from twelve-and-six?

But he was an apprentice. An apprentice at Wickers. He told everybody and they were impressed. He could tell.

It was on that day that Allan mentioned it. The trip down the river that week-end.

'Ahm nee sailor. Ah wouldn't hev went, but Col said it

would be a new experience. It was.' Allan obviously didn't enjoy that new experience.

What was that new experience? Tom had to know.

Oh. So Mister Timpson had a new boat? That was interesting. Tom wondered about that new boat. Perhaps he could get a ride in it? What length would it be? Was it carvel or clinker-built? Was it just a converted lifeboat? Did it have a real marine engine? Did it have a straight-through reverse? Did it have real brass portholes? All these were very important things. None of those things meant anything to Allan. He had been seasick. No more jolly-jack-tar for him.

His Da hadn't got to get up so early these days. He didn't work at Hebburn any more. He was right here with Tom at Elswick. Just across the watter from Gateshead.

The truth of the matter was an inevitability that drifted to him. He'd wondered why his Da wasn't so interested in the boat these days. He'd said he was too tired now that he was working. It was also true that the touch of gas he'd got in the war was playing him up. Trips in the open air were supposed to do him good. But they weren't.

He and his Da were working. Mister Timpson had a new boat and was nice to Tom. Tom thought that Mister Timpson was almost as good as Nelson Eddy. He'd said it to anybody who wanted to know, 'Mister Timpson looks a lot like Nelson Eddy.' Anybody who looked like Nelson Eddy must be a good chap.

Putting it all together, he'd discovered how clever his Da really was. Just like Allan Philips, he knew there was going to be another war. He'd sacrificed his boat for Tom. The boat that had taken him hundreds of back-breaking hours to build.

Mister Timpson now had that smart little cruiser and young Tom was safe from that war that loomed ahead. Safe from places where you buried yor mates and used their graves as back-rests. Places where even the dirty black watter of the Gut would taste sweet by comparison. Tom would never have to take to Woodbines.

He was now indeed a bound apprentice. He had that huge stiff piece of paper to prove it. Even the Government couldn't prise him loose from that. They didn't want to. As Allan had said, 'There's them that'll git shot, and them that'll not!'

A rift suddenly appeared between all parties. Tom wondered about it. He could sense a change in atmosphere. It started when Col said, 'Aye, Tom's comin' on fine. His last job was a picture.'

Mister Timpson had enjoined, 'Don't praise them too much, it's bad for them!' Maybe he was right. But Col knew Tom better than Mister Timpson. He was there at the foundry only three days a week and he had those other two foundries to look after. Things weren't so friendly any more.

Just by accident he discovered 'his boat', now Mister Timpson's boat, half sunk at a nearby mooring. The bow had been stove in; not a lot but enough to start the forward planks. She was leaking like a sieve. It was a sorry sight and Tom felt sick. Did that Mister Timpson really look like Nelson Eddy?

One of Allan's balance-weight moulds blew up! It went up like a miniature volcano. Somebody had accidently plugged the core vents. When this happens, generated gases find their own way out, back through the molten iron; hence the volcanic effect.

Half-a-dozen fires broke out from the hundreds of flying molten metal droplets. Everybody on the casting floor broke sprint records, then they returned to fight the volcano the only way they knew how, with strategically thrown shovelfuls of sand. The combined weight soon damped down that spouting runner-box.

The fire-brigade came racing in to the foundry to tackle

the many fires. Miraculously no one was seriously burned. Lots had little pinholes in their clothes and it seemed incredible that such an explosion could hurt only the crane man. It also hurt somebody's ego.

Allan was the royal so he had to take the blame. Tom knew it would be his mate's fault. That fella Blackie, he would be the one; he wasn't in Allan's class.

There was an inquest. Hard words were spoken. Accusations made and rejected. When you were best, you got the worst criticism.

Mister Timpson had a lot to say, 'Twenty firemen, Head Office on the war-path, crane man burned, production stopped, careless work.'

Allan didn't care much for the careless work bit; he was never careless.

Mister Timpson didn't look like Nelson Eddy any more.

Col had the ultimate solution. It ended all the arguments. 'If you can dee it better yor-sel, Mister Timpson, dee it!'

All foundry managers retreated from such objective terms.

PART SIX

Apprenticeship

'It must have been sabotage!' Dan exclaimed, as they excitedly discussed the hair-raising event of yesterday.

'Sabotage?' Tom's eyes widened in amazement. Spies? Spies here in Wickers? That was interesting.

The older apprentices scoffed at that.

'Silly bugger, Dan! The vents got clogged, that's all. Blackie used too much wet loam on the core-prints. He's a tear-arse just like you.' The speaker laughed. 'Spies, they wouldn't risk comin' inta the foundry, we'd set their arses afire.'

Yes, that was a logical explanation about Blackie and the vents. Tom agreed with that because he was learning fast.

But logical explanations weren't as exciting as spies in the factory. He'd keep an eye open for spies. Just let them try to spoil his job.

Dan's theory sparked off Tom's memory. he recalled those funny fellas who, even as he spoke, might be spying on them. Them funny fellas who were from Europe, Garmins, he suspected.

Those fellas were making a 'dig' in old Redheugh Hall. The local haunted house, to the children in the Teams area of Gateshead.

The old Redheugh Hall was situated between Tom's old school and the River Tyne. It occupied a site which sloped down to the river. As long as Tom could remember the old hall had been surrounded by a robust fence of old railway sleepers.

Obviously the old hall was haunted. Everybody knew that. Tom wouldn't dare climb that big black ominous wall which loomed threateningly against inquisitive children. As he grew up, he still wasn't sure about that old place.

It was alright to pass by the old hall in the daytime, but at night you had to sprint like mad just in case a ghostly gadgy reached out and grabbed you.

Next to the hall were the 'bankies'. They were the Teams St. Moritz in the winter. The best route for sledging was hard by that ominous black fence. Ghosts didn't come out in the winter. Like flies, they only came out in the summer.

Tom still had his sledge. The sledge that his Da had made for him. It was made with the same thoroughness his Da made everything.

That sledge could hold four people, if you called children people. Everybody said it looked like a 'bought' one. You could imagine it being pulled by a team of dogs with 'you know who' shouting, 'Mush!' That was the term those fellas he'd seen on the pictures used to encourage their team of dogs.

He'd tried to introduce Johnnie's dog, Prince, as lead dog, but he thought nothing of that. He could and would pull that sledge easily when the runners were nice and bright; but as soon as Tom sat on it, that doggy engine stopped and looked back with a sour expression that needed little interpretation.

But it was summer now and no frozen snow covered the bankies. Instead they had a thick coating of lush grass, except for the sledging-skiing track. It was summer and two funny fellas had come to Gateshead. All the way from Europe they had come to bring light to the folks of Gateshead. They were fair-haired and very nice. They were also, Garmins!

At first it was rumoured they were digging for gold. Digging in the grounds of the old hall for some lost treasure. There was yet another rumour that they were digging in the grounds of the old hall for parts of the old Roman Wall. If they were they were digging on the wrong side of the river. Gateshead was situated on the South side of the River Tyne while the famous wall was built on the North side. But they were Garmins, how would they know any better?

One of those Garmins was called Feedle Funph and the other Feedle Dee. At least that's what the children called them. They made much of the local children.

The ladies of the district took good care of them, providing tea, cakes and scones. They were two God-like visitors from another planet, in Gateshead to do good work.

Tom did just give the area of the dig a courtesy visit, to see what all the excitement was about. He was disgusted to see certain local girls almost fawning upon those two blond giants. Lasses were daft! Ellen Poster was there, he gave her a frown. He got a smile in return. She said, 'Hello, Tombo!' That took him back.

Those two affable Garmins didn't fool Tom. He knew all about Garmins from his Da and Barney and his Granda. Bella, his Grandma, after the death of her eldest son, Thomas, in the Great War, she would have all Garmins shot on sight. Still, those two nice blond fellas didn't look at all like villains.

But again, Tom wasn't fooled by them. There was something distinctly odd about two fellas who would come all the way from Europe to a place like Gateshead, which had been described by some half-wits as, 'a dirty back-lane leading to Newcastle.' What was so important about Gateshead?

As he stood in the grounds of that famous 'Reedheugh Hall' Tom pondered the matter. Years ago he'd never have dared to climb those ominous-looking railway sleepers. Now a lot of them were gone. Stolen for firewood. His Uncle

Jos had been chased by the local slop for such an offence. He was never caught, being so fleet of foot, but there was always a 'copper's nark' about. Jos Dobson was put on probation.

But here he was now standing on that hallowed ground and looking right across the river into where he worked, the great armaments factory. It was true, those two funny fellas with their good Garmin binoculars could see right into Wickers from the opposite bank of the river. What sort of gold could they discover on this site?

Tom was sure that they could see the tanks being water-tested outside the tank shop. Fortunately they couldn't see Tom and Dan sunning themselves on the top of the new air-raid shelters being brought into the foundry for the war now expected. That was most important; they might tell the dreaded Col.

The iron and brass foundry was tucked away around the bend in the river. Out of sight of those two gold diggers. All they'd be able to see from their site at Redheugh Hall would be the power pylons leading from Dunston power station into Tom's foundry. They wouldn't be able to see Tom, Dan and the others when they sneaked out onto the gantry to get a breath of fresh air after the day's cast. That was a relief.

Tom, Dan and the other apprentices, encouraged by Dan's uncle who was the labourers' charge-man, helped to fill the sandbags that would cover those new air-raid shelters. It was the usual competition as to who could fill most in the least time. Dan and Tom would compete as usual and after the first fifty or so they regretted volunteering, their finger tips being raw with the rough heavy bags. They were glad when all the bags were filled and packed away on and around the air-raid shelters. If it was hard work it was exciting fun. When standing on those bags on top of that air-raid shelter, you could see those girls in that factory over the line, that much better.

And if those Garmins digging in Reedheugh Hall were spies, Dan and Swan and Tom and the others couldn't be seen from that spot.

Not that they could be spies, those funny fellas. It was as Bill Wilson had said, Allan Philips' job had blown up because the vents were clogged. But how did they get clogged? That incident had shocked Allan more than anyone. He'd remember it better than his birthday.

Tom had thought of telling Col about those Garmins digging in the old hall. Thinking was about as far as he got. He had a fair idea what Col would say about the fanciful dreams of apprentices. He'd already offered suggestions on production to Col, who had smiled and had said, 'That's the way, lad, keep tryin', but that was invented twenty years ago!' Col had been there before.

They continued finding bits from the explosion over the next few days. The new balance-weight mould was ready for casting and Col and Mr. Timpson were hovering. They didn't want to interfere but showed their concern by being there when the mould was 'closed' and made ready for casting.

'Never seen so many gaffers!' Allan grumbled as he checked and re-checked everything.

There was a general lull in the foundry as the ladle full of molten iron was brought to Allan's mould. A mould that had never before received such attention. The crane man, the pourer, the ladle steadier and the 'skimmer' all had an unusual and undeniable sweat on at the thought of what could again occur.

It was Allan's mate Blackie who lowered the tension. He stepped forward. 'Ah'll pour the bugger me-sel!' he announced.

The regular ladle man waved him away. He wasn't going to have it said that he was afraid, even if he was.

He gave his hand signals for centre to the crane driver, now equipped with brand-new blue glasses; he at least was taking no chances.

The hypnotic fiery liquid was aimed and introduced to the mould runner-box and it flowed down and into the mould without a splash. Credit due to he who controlled the ladle. He hadn't lost his nerve.

An unusual silence fell on the foundry as the molten iron flowed. A silence so keen they could hear the liquid iron running in and around the mould. They could hear the noise of the birth of a new shape. They could hear the rush and the noise of gases being generated. They counted the vents; they were all working. Smiles were exchanged as those vents lit with a W-O-O-F from the high temperature ladle. It would be alright now. Confidence and esteem were restored.

Blackie would now be free to get drunk in the pub on Scotswood Road and brag about the things he'd done and the things he'd seen. Who could blame him? This was a time of celebration; he needed only half an excuse and now he had full reason for that beery celebration. When he had a skinful he would build moulds and castings so big they'd need permission from the landlord to knock the pub wall down to get them out. That would be the time to call, 'Time gentlemen, please!'

Scotswood Road had many pubs; all with appropriate names. The Moulders Arms, The Patent Hammer, The Mechanics, haunts of the various craftsmen who sought to quench their thirst after a hard day at Wickers; easy meat for eager secret ears.

Tom decided not to tell Col about those Garmins digging in the grounds of Redheugh Hall. He was growing up and growing out of that impressionable age of Sister Winnie stories. No! Those Garmins were just digging to find Roman remains. Some old fort erected on the South side of the river.

He just wondered? Would Ellen Poster like him if he dyed his hair blond and wore short pants like those blond giants?

Big Guns

It was a chance remark from Lang Jack that again brought forth the rivalry and in that the effect of the explosion began to dim.

Jack had remarked, wisely, 'We'll need plenty of them anti-aircraft guns now. The next war will be fought in the air.'

Dan agreed. 'Aye, we'll need aal the three-point-seven-fives we can make. That's why Col and Mr. Timpson was givin' Allan's job so much attention. They's caalin' out for them from the top office.'

'Who says they's three-point-seven-fives?' Tom fired back. 'Ain't they four-point-fives?'

'Course not! Everybody knows they's three-point-seven-fives.' Dan said it with such confidence, it must be so.

That silenced Tom. He was sure that he'd heard somebody say those guns were four-point-fives. Had he heard it while in Col's office? He was making Col's tea now. Every day he went into Col's office and picked up his little tea-pot, already with a tea spoon of new tea in it. He'd take that to the communal boiler for filling with boiling water.

Each and every Friday without fail, there'd be a shiny bronze threepenny bit waiting for him. Col was a most methodical man. If the telephone rang while Tom was in the office and Col was out, Tom would take the message. Is that where he'd heard about, four-point-fives?

'Anyway, if they was four-point-fives, they wouldn't be the biggest guns in the factory, aah've seen the real biggun's, the fifteen inchers!' Dan waited for the silence that would follow such an announcement.

He had seen the fifteen inch guns? It was unbelievable.

But had Dan seen them? And if he had, he should have kept such information to himself.

'I'll take you Tom, if you want to see them?' Dan looked at Jack. 'You'd better not come, Jack. You can't run fast enough; besides, yor the only one that looks like you in the works.'

Jack was crestfallen. He hid that. 'Me? Ah don't want to look at guns. Them's only for little lads like you. Aye, take young Tom. Ah've got more important things to do. A fella wants a bit of peace at bait time.'

They had rushed through their bait. Hadn't even thought to go down to the river, through the pump house, to throw their usual few flat stones. Five skids across the top of the water was the current record.

It had to be something special to make them rush through their tea and sandwiches. It was. This was the day that Dan was taking Tom on a tour of the works. They had to be on their way quick to get back to their work in time for the last buzzer.

They brushed their overalls. They didn't want to look too much like raggy mats. They carried their tool of office, a smoothing trowel, in the rule pocket of their overall. That made them look important. They were craftsmen, weren't they?

In next to no time they were out of the foundry and up the 'yard' and past the Head Office. When they were opposite this Dan said, 'Them buggers just sits on their arses. They's non-producers!'

'Is this it?' Tom had asked the same question two or three times as they travelled on. Wickers was a very large factory and like a rabbit warren. The foundry had been the start of Armstrongs' great enterprise. Indeed, the wall of the original chapel was still part of the foundry. The 'chapel' was the haunt of the blacksmith. Tom could still remember his first days in the foundry; when he'd been sent with the furnace-man's tools for re-tipping. 'Take them to the blacksmith, lad,' he'd been instructed. The blacksmith? The chapel? He asked Col.

'That's where the great Lord Armstrong started this factory, Tom. They say he bought this old chapel on the banks of the River Tyne. He was a great success, so they say. He made the money and got the credit, we did the work.'

Dan kept saying, 'No,' and Tom began to wonder if Dan knew the layout of Wickers as well as he bragged.

'Oh aye! Ah've been here before. We's got to dodge about a bit, got to watch out for the fireman gadgies.'

The 'fireman' gadgies, they doubled as security men in Wickers. Ah, Tom had it now. So that's why Dan hadn't invited Jack. He couldn't run as fast as Tom and Dan, should they have to run from a fireman gadgy. Tom wasn't feeling too confident now.

The firemen were at certain strategic points. The apprentice grapevine had most places plotted. Security men were no match for agile young lads.

'This is it!' Dan hissed triumphantly. 'Through this little steel door.' He cautiously tried the door handle; it opened freely.

'These places are a lot cleaner than the foundry.' Dan was whispering now. They entered the big building. It was like a cathedral. It sounded empty, the workmen here were also having their bait.

All their former bravado was gone now. They had a feeling two scruffy foundry apprentices had no right in such a clinical church-like atmosphere. But after all, they were bound apprentices, at least Dan was; Tom was on the way, being sixteen. They should have nothing to fear; they were part of the system and they had their moulders' trowels stuck in their overalls, hadn't they.

They picked up courage and sauntered on. Best to look guiltless. The workmen taking bait in various corners hardly gave them a second glance.

'There they are!' Dan hissed, nudging Tom. He pointed ahead and there they were, those magnetic big guns. They hurried forward past a great empty circular pit and on to yet another, this one filled with a huge turret.

They stopped and gazed open-mouthed. The size of those great guns took their inquisitive breath away. They gawped unashamedly.

'Aye, and what are you two little buggers up to?' a gruff voice behind them demanded.

It was a fair cop. The fireman had been waiting for them, so it appeared to them. They were rooted to the spot. How could they answer? Dan recovered first, he was the oldest.

'We was just lookin' at wor work, mister!'

Tom took up that theme. It was a good one.

'Aye, we was interested in wor castin's. We make balance-weights for them guns.' That wasn't quite true, but it was enough to blunt any official thrust. Tom knew enough about the system to conclude that a security guard wouldn't know one casting from another. He was right.

The uniformed giant looked down at those now red-faced culprits.

'You two? You make what, for these guns?' It was a puzzlement. Could it be true? He was after all not concerned with production.

'Aye, balance-weights! We work with Allan Philips. He's the top craftsman.' It seemed silly to mention that Allan's castings were for smaller guns.

It was enough to stop officialdom in its tracks. It wasn't every day that young craftsmen came to examine their work.

'You shouldn't be here! Neebody's allowed in here! Didn't you see the notice?' The blue sleeve pointed back to the door.

'Aye, but that's nowt to dee with us? We work here! We's apprentices!' Dan blurted it out. That was the way to do it. He stuck his chest out.

They'd been joined by a man in a white coat. A white coat like Col's. A gaffer?

'They say they came from the foundry to look at their work.' The blue uniform winked at the foreman.

The group was joined by other now grinning workmen.

The foreman, keeping his face straight, said, 'Come to look at their work, that's commendable, but are you sure they are from the foundry? They might be spies. Garmin spies in disguise?'

They knew they weren't spies. But 'commendable'? What did that mean? Was that good or bad? They both protested their innocence.

'We's not spies! We work with Mister Col! He's the top man in Wickers.' It was time to bring out their big guns. Everyone knew Mister Col, so they thought. But this man did.

'Ah, yor Mister Col's lads?'

'Aye, Mister Col said that every good craftsman follows up his work.' Tom did the talking. He felt the tension had eased.

'Will them guns shoot to Sou' Shields, Mister?' It was time to change the subject.

'Aye! Course they will!' The man in the white coat grinned at the man in blue. 'Want to have a go?'

Dan and Tom grinned in embarrassment. Dan took out his smoothing trowel and smoothed at some invisible mould. Tom gazed at his feet. Somebody was trying to pull their leg.

'Garn! They's pointed the wrong way. They'd hit King Geordie's bridge afore they hit Sou' Shields.' They couldn't fool Tom.

The man in white looked at the man in blue. Others had gathered to see the fun. The foreman's bluff had been called.

'Harry!' The foreman cupped his hands to project his voice. A man popped his head out of a scuttle on the side of the huge turret.

'Aye, Bill?'

'Harry, give us some elevation and prepare to shoot one

round ower the New Bridge. Make sure you lock on to Sou' Shields Town Hall.'

Harry gazed down on the group. It wasn't every day he got an order to lock on to South Shields Town Hall.

'Blank, solid, high explosive, armour piercin'. What sorta round do you want?'

All eyes focused on the two hapless lads.

'It's yor choice, lads!' the foreman said. 'Tell Harry.'

The lads were frozen stiff. The spotlight of responsibility rooted them to the floor. It was a time when the tongue became a stone in those normally cheeky mouths.

Somewhere down in the bowels of that huge turret an engine hummed into life. Bells rung and the huge mass started to move around. The huge barrels began to tilt upward; they wouldn't hit King Geordie's bridge now.

Tom was first to recover. He knew about shooting; he'd just bought an air-pistol.

'Garn, you's havin' us on! You need a firearm certificate to fire that thing! You can't fire that gun over a public highway.' He looked triumphantly at Dan. That was one over Dan. He didn't know that.

'Ready to shoot!' Came a voice from somewhere.

Dan was open-mouthed; he prepared to run. Silence descended on the work-shop. The crane-men in their lofty transport moved with a quiet rumble behind those three tall threatening tubes. They were getting into the act.

'Who's name goes doon for this shell?' a voice enquired.

'What's yor names, lads?' the foreman asked.

It was shattering. Did these men actually intend to fire on Sou' Shields Toon Hall? It was unbelievable. They weren't going to be responsible for that.

'What's yor names, lads?' the foreman asked again, having some difficulty keeping a straight face.

'Ah'm Buck Jones and he's Tom Mix!' Tom yelled and pushed Dan towards the door. They went through at top speed.

They didn't stop running till the foundry doors came in sight.

'Them fellas was only kiddin'!' Dan pumped for breath. 'You didn't hear a bang, did you?'

Tom didn't speak. He felt distinctly foolish. Their actions he now felt were too foolish to laugh at. Being conned by them fellas into believing they'd actually fire a shot from those big guns.

Consulting with Allan Philips about the matter. Not telling all of course. Not the whole story, he was now not so sure one way or the other.

'Oh aye, Armstrong us'ta take his early breech-loaders doon to the cliffs at Tynemouth and have a go there.'

'But how do they test our big guns? Them guns they has up in the gun shop? They don't take them to Tynemouth, do they?' The oracle would know the answer.

'Whey no, Tom. They's too big to cart aboot. They just fire a shell or two, say, ower Sou' Shields. They don't hit Sou' Shields of course. They fires ower the top, at a target out at sea.' It was said with a deadpan expression.

It was a joke that could be carried for months. But, did them fellas really intend to shoot, ower Sou' Shields Toon Hall?

Drawing up the Future

It was obvious that most in the foundry knew about their visit to the gun-shop. The downright sniggers from the other apprentices and quiet grins from the mature craftsmen proved the story had spread. It was a time for two adventurers to keep their heads down.

Personal pride was a buoyancy factor second to none. Danny became fierce with Jack when he scoffed at their visit.

'Garn, you'd never find the little bits that you make for that big gun!' Jack grinned at Allan Philips, dodging about his moulding box as usual. They were all four gathered at that usual focal point.

Danny's fists clenched. What should never be done to Danny was to question his work. Work was a religion to Danny. He had to do well; his father had brayed it into him. He was doing well but needed assurance. He was ready to lash out at Jack.

Allan Philips came to his rescue. He winked at Tom ... 'You lads got nowt to dee? For want of a nail, the kingdom was lost! Nail's a little thing.'

'Eh?' asked Jack wonderingly.

'It's the little things that's important. Big things is nee good without little things!' They moved as the great man moved about his mould.

Danny beamed at that. This was the stuff he wanted to hear. His fists were still ready if Lang Jack wanted trouble.

'Who said that?' Jack asked, eyeing the aggressive Danny.

'Me!' Allan said as he moved Tom's resting foot off his moulding box. 'You lads got nowt to dee?'

The lads grinned sheepishly. There was plenty 'to dee' but nothing was better than listening to this teddy-bearish philosopher.

'For want of a nail the shoe was lost, for want of the shoe the horse was lost. If you had a spare horse in King Dick's time, you could have half his kingdom.' Tom and Danny got that teddy-bear nose wrinkled in their direction.

'Why no, man, you's all mixed up!' Jack grinned down on the others. 'It was Ben Franklin said that. It had nowt to dee with Richard the Third. You'd have known that if you'd went to night-school, like me.' Jack almost stuck his chest out at beating the old master.

'Amounts to the same thing.' Allan almost forgot himself, he put up his foot on to the moulding box. It was down in an instant as he busied about. It gave him a few seconds to combat Jack.

'It means that even kings is knackered if their horse has nee nail in its shoe. Them big guns would be knackered without Danny's little castin's. But just think, little things is most important, we build great-big guns, just to kill, little people. So there yar, little things is more important than big things.' He moved around his job brushing them aside like the chaff they were.

The other three stood back in respect. The interview had come to an end. They drifted back to their work, feeling more important than yesterday.

Tom said, 'You larns nowt at night-school; only daft things like Jack said. Ah could have gone to the Central School but they's got a lot of cissies there. They wear daft uniforms. My cousin Bella, she and her mate Edie Pallas goes there; the lads caals them Central Sausages but they's more like black and white puddin's.' Tom laughed as he recalled his cousin and her friend running the gauntlet every day through a hail of catcalls.

He'd passed his exams, when he was eleven years old, to allow him to go to that Grammar School, but the uniforms and facing the possible derision of the local lads had found him lacking. He had to admit that his cousin Bella was braver than he.

When his apprenticeship papers were signed, he found he would get another sixpence a week if he went to night-school.

His Da said he should. The major-domo thought sixpence more a week was not to be sneered at.

'What should ah dee, Allan?' he asked the fountain.

'Get yor-sel to night-school! Larn aal you can. You could be a manager one day. Wickers ain't the only place on earth.'

Tom was beginning to think that Wickers was the only place on earth. He beat a path to Wickers every morning at the same time. True it was work, work, but it was interesting work in which he could compete with Danny. Paid to do things he liked to do ... What could be better than that?

But could he be a manager one day, like Mr. Timpson? Maybe it was worth going to night-school after all.

They all pushed him to go to night-school. His Ma, his Da, Allan Philips and Mr. Timpson. Mr Col. was uncommitted, Tom wondered why. Jack said, 'Whey aye man, larn yor 'trig' and you'll be in the R.A.F. straight away when the war comes.'

So, not only could he be a manager, he could become a pilot in the R.A.F.? This night-school business could be worth looking into.

Danny thought it was a waste of time! He said as much. 'How can them teachers larn you aboot foundry work? They knaas nowt. None of them could hold a job doon in the foundry. It's like that fella said, 'Them as does, does it, others just taaks aboot it.' Did Mr. Col hold the same view?

Nevertheless he did go to night-school and with mixed feelings. He found it slightly boring. His teacher thought he was bright. Tom felt anything but bright. Coming home from a hard day's work in the foundry, dirty and sticky, needed reward. Going to the pics was his usual reward. Now he had to give that up. Give it up for subjective mental work he felt had no immediate benefit.

He was used to immediate benefit. In his world you did your work and you got your reward, even if that reward was only the satisfaction of producing a good useful casting.

He was pretty good at maths, but found that subject most odd. Adding, subtracting, multiplying, dividing things that didn't exist, he found a waste of time. English was boring; however give him a pencil, a rule, compasses and a set of angles and he would draw plan, section and projection with an interest he never had in those other two subjects. If this activity did not have the very same attraction and satisfaction as making moulds to fill with molten metal, at least it was creative in the primary sense.

He passed his first night-school exam! True he wasn't first-class at maths or English but he got a first with a distinction in technical drawing. His teacher was more pleased than he. Favouritism, somebody said.

For passing his exam he'd get another sixpence in his pay-packet every week. On the strength of that he resolved to enroll for the second year night-school. It was either a manager's job or a pilot in the R.A.F.; he wasn't sure which he'd choose.

His teacher proved how pleased he was by advising his employer that, 'Thomas is so good at drawing, he should be transferred to the drawing office.'

'Thomas' He was living in another world. 'Before lang,' remarked Jack, 'we'll have to pay half-a-dollar to taak to him.'

It was a short-lived flight into dreamland. The letter from Captain Tinn brought him back to cold reality. The letter was a reply to the letter sent by his teacher to Wickers' management. It was short and sour.

'In reply to your letter, we know what is best for our apprentices!' A letter so precise and terse as to be rude.

His teacher was livid. His professional advice ignored as if of no consequence, he made it plain he'd never interfere with Wickers' system again. Tom felt he was responsible for it all. It was his ambition that had caused his teacher's bitterness.

He attended the next session of night-school for two weeks, then quit. He felt an outcast. He was lacking in some way. He'd let his teacher down by not getting that job in the drawing office. If it was true his drawing was first-class, it followed he wasn't good enough in some other way. What other way?

He asked Mister Col why 'they' wouldn't have him in the drawing office. It was, after all, Mister Col who wasn't keen on that night-school.

'Why will they not have you in the drawing office, son? Ah don't know, but ah could guess. Maybe you's green instead of blue. Maybe you part yor hair on the wrong side. Maybe you live on the wrong side of the river? Aye, but this management's not daft. You's a good moulder or have the makin's of one. But you's all tied up legally as an apprentice moulder. Ah know you thinks they's all against you, but the facts are, any silly bugger can draw lines on paper, but how many can match Dan and you and what you do in the foundry?'

It was all Greek to Tom in his present state. In addition he'd heard that Mister Timpson's son, who'd spent some time in the foundry, he was going into the drawing office. Tom liked John, they were in the same sea-scout troop, an activity engineered by Mister Timpson to give Tom an interest in the boating he'd lost by the sale of his Da's boat.

It was beginning to look very unfair. What was the point of studying if all the 'good jobs' went to the bosses sons?

He caught Mister Col in his office one day when he went in to get his tea-pot. He appeared in a benign mood so he brought up the subject of favouritism.

Mister Col gave him a quizzical look. 'How did you get yor job, Tom? There's scores outside would like yor job. If yor Da had to mek a choice, would he pick his own lad, course he would. The drawin' office is the best place for John; he'd never make a good moulder. You and Dan, yor good at yor work, aye, and because yor good at yor work, you'll never be a foreman, just like ah'll never be a manager. Head foreman is as far as ah'll get.' It became a time of dual confession. They parted knowing each other better.

He'd been plagued by new ideas. New ways of doing this and that. The old hands frowned on new ways. The old ways were good enough for them. They said so.

'Ee lad, you'll put us aal oot of our jobs!'

Allan Philips scoffed at them. He was a man of no vices.

'Ah could dee an hour's work while them lazy buzzers (Allan never swore) filled their pipes. If they got paid for pipe fillin' and pipe smokin' ...'

'But they does,' laughed Tom.

Allan joined him in that laughter. 'Aye, ah suppose they does. So tek no notice of them. You get on with yor drawin's and yor ideas. You'll be drivin' up to see us one day in yor Rolls-Royce, I'll be bound.'

Tom got an opportunity to excerise his growing curiosity sooner than expected. He had for some time plagued some of the furnace men as to why he and Dan and company had to retreat out on to the gantry to escape the clouds of black smoke that issued from the crucible furnaces. One said, growled, 'Mind yor own business!' Another was more helpful.

The incident that sparked off Tom's idea for a new type of furnace happened not in the morning when the furnaces were cold, but in the afternoon when the crucible furnaces were at their highest and fiercest temperature.

It was time when Smithy the furnace man, Snowball, disappeared to the tune of a roaring bang and in a sea of flame and black smoke.

Snowball got his name from the white undershirt he wore while tending his furnaces. That and his close-cropped white hair would be all that could be seen above the roaring white-hot flames as he dashed in and out feeding the pots till full. His sparkling reflection in the flames would dim as his hair and shirt also dimmed with their covering of sweat and grime. He would appear again on Monday, as white as snow. There were those who swore they could tell what day it was by the colour of Smithy's undershirt.

It was true that Smithy was a mighty worker. A tear-arse so it was claimed by some who also claimed he did enough work for two, thus, 'kept some other poor sod out of a job'.

Tom thought how fortunate that 'poor sod' must have been, in not having such a job. Smithy's job was one of the hottest and dirtiest he had ever seen. He wondered and marvelled how a man could work in such conditions.

Somebody said, 'He sweats so much, there's no poison in his body.' Tom could well believe that.

Nevertheless, that great tough character disappeared into what looked like Dante's Inferno. In an instant the foundry was filled with black smoke which drove them all out to seek fresh air. Then somebody remembered Smithy. Despite the danger, in they went to find him staggering around; still trying to do his duty and feed those hungry crucibles.

It took all of thirty minutes to clear the foundry of smoke. The fire-engine couldn't get into the foundry to fight that fire because of the dense smoke. Eventually they all came back into the foundry and got on with the job. Everybody came to look at the source of the trouble; the loading platform from which Snowball fed those furnaces.

But what had happened to Snowball, was he burned alive? The rumours were many. The truth was simple; he was in the first-aid station, from which he appeared two hours later. He was well singed and still in shock, but still intent on doing his duty.

Some thought that insistence to duty remarkable. Others thought and said, 'Bugger's afraid somebody else might get his job.'

They all had their theories about what had happened. Dan knew the answer. 'He'll have shovelled in a live roond with aal them other cartridge cases. Them big half-inch cartridges can blaa a hole in the pot.'

It was true enough. The crucible had burst at its bottom and spilled the molten bronze into the furnace, the bronze then running out of the back of the furnace at the injection hole. Snowball's loading platform had beneath it a labyrinth of air-pipes and fuel lines well covered with a liberal coating of coal-tar and brass cuttings. Snowball was on piecework, hence the clutter beneath his loading platform.

It was also true that on occasion the metal charge could be

thousands of empty brass cartridge cases, among which could be found very occasionally, a live round. These were mostly .303 type. As Dan had said, there could be the other bigger type, the half-inch. Was it one of these that had found its way into that molten bronze?

Tom didn't think that was the answer. In his obersvation cartridge cases always went into the pot first. Whatever had caused the explosion had gone into the pot last and when the pot was almost full of molten bronze. He said nothing about his theory, knowing it might cause some hurt to a favourite person.

The explosion concentrated his mind on his new idea for a furnace. The molten bronze flowing back out of the furnace and setting fire to the fuel system he thought was an area of thought to be explored. But how had Snowball escaped death? He put it to the foundry philosopher.

'How did Smithy walk away from that? Ah don't know, Tom. But God moves in mysterious ways his wonders to perform. Maybe Smithy is one of God's key men; one of them that has to keep on meltin' the metal that meks us aal.' He gave Tom one of his famous mysterious smiles, just like the one he gave when Tom asked about those big guns.

Everything and everybody in the foundry was covered with soot. A sort of black rain. If the men could wash it off, it hung about the foundry for days. Col's office was one place that had escaped the black coating. It was also a place for passing confidences. Tom waited until he saw Mister Col hang up his trilby and expose that shiny dome. Funnily, he didn't mind if Tom saw him without his hat; was that a sign of trust, or was it that Tom was still only a boy and therefore of little consequence?

He quickly came to the point. He brought his drawings from under the bib of his overalls, secreted there against prying, mocking eyes.

Mister Col ran his experienced eyes over those neat lines.

He absorbed the legends. He listened while Tom poured out his theory. Tom stood back and waited for his words to have effect. How would Mister Col react? Already he was wishing he hadn't bothered. If he was good at drawing, he wasn't quite so good at explanations. He wasn't yet aware that some people cannot construe drawing, in the same manner that some people are colour blind.

It was less than a minute before Mister Col spoke. Seconds that seemed like a lifetime to this young innovator.

'Aye, aye, these are good clear drawin's. It looks very interesting'. Ah see yor tekin' an interest on the things you see around you. Best thing for you to dee, Tom, is to submit it to the management. See what they have to say.' He gave Tom a smile of encouragement and Tom swept up his precious drawings and stammered his way out of the great man's presence. He got ten paces away then remembered he'd gone into the office to get Col's tea-pot. He turned back and re-entered that now friendly little office. He grabbed up that little pot but before he got back through the door, Col said, 'You can mention my name when you send it in.

The next half-hour was a blur to Tom. That he could mention Col's name, that was almost like being patted on the head by God.

He'd folded his drawings carefully, almost reverendly. Along with a letter with a few words of explantion, he put them in a large envelope and addressed it to Wickers Ltd, Elswick Scotswood Road, Newcastle upon Tyne. He waited for the bombshell that he knew would happen. It would only take twenty-four hours for the management to read his letter, then it would happen. They would see the great mistake they had made in not putting him in the drawing office when his teacher had advised it.

He'd about given up hope after the second and third day. After all, the Head Office was only 150 yards away; only a telephone call away; perhaps his drawings had been lost in the post. The many facets of failure grew before him.

It was on Friday, four days after the management must have received his letter, that he saw that well-dressed fella with the ginger hair come into the foundry and go to Col's office. Tom had seen him before, this slim-jim of the ginger hair who always had a hanky in the breast pocket of his posh suit. He was one of the top brains in Wickers. Even higher than Mr. Timpson. It must be something important to bring him down to the dirty foundry.

They came out of Col's office and stood for a while. Tom knew that Col was pointing him out without appearing to do so. They went back in again and shortly afterwards the well-dressed slim-jim-ginger fella came out with Col and they both walked to the exit door bent in earnest conversation.

'Must be something up,' Dan muttered in his ear. 'Somebody must be mekin' too many badun's. That's what's brought him doon here.'

Mr. Ginger-slim-jim's entry into the foundry disturbed both Dan and Tom. Tom saw it as a good omen but Dan as a bad one. Freddy Gee growled, 'Them buggers always brings trouble. It's either cut the prices or pay some poor bugger off.'

Freddy Gee led a well-ordered life. He'd been at Wickers forever. Today, tomorrow and yesterday all meant the same to him. Sight of that freshly ironed white collar encircled by a well-disciplined tie with Windsor knot might send him running to the shop steward in panic.

Freddy also wore a tie to distinguish him as a craftsman. It was a yesterday, today and tomorrow tie. It never varied in colour, character or shape. It was neither dirty nor clean. It had a well-ordered gloomy durability.

It was almost a nail-biting week-end. Mister Col had said nothing to him that last Friday. All day that next Monday he also had nothing to say. When Tom got home that Monday night there was a letter waiting for him, from Wickers. He was almost afraid to open it. Would he be up in the clouds, or down among the dead men?

The reply was short and to the point. 'We thank you for your letter. We have had our experts look at your idea but they consider that it would be impractical and therefore is of no interest to this company. We again must thank you for your interest.' He was down among the dead men.

Full of gloom he showed the letter to Mister Col the next day. 'They say my idea's nee good.' He waited for consolation. Would Col be in on it? Would he have already known the content of the letter?

What does anyone with experience who also had suffered disappointment say to an innocent?

'Aye, there's them that say that there's nee greater pain than the pain of a new idea, lad. Yor askin' Wickers to swim again the tide of convention. Tek a look outside, son; there's some fellas out there who want nee more out of life than a pipe-full of baccy. The management here is nee better.'

Tom stood and listened. It seemed the right and only thing to do. Here was a man who understood. Had perhaps gone through the same disappointing experiences?

'There's some good fellas in here,' he ventured. 'There's Allan Philips, for one.'

Mister Col looked up at him and smiled. 'Aye, Allan's not a bad fella. He's a damn good worker. But y'naa, fellas like him, aal they want is work. Work they understand is aal they want. Try to get fellas like him to change their ways, just try. Fellas like him can't see further than next week's pay-packet.'

Tom was amazed. Here was one of his closest friends being reduced before his eyes. It was worse than finding out that Mr. Timpson didn't look like Nelson Eddy any more. His picture of the world was changing.

'Why would Wickers not take up my idea?' He blurted it out to this man he was getting to know better than before.

'Why would they not take it up, son? I've just told you. Yor fellow man doesn't like change, besides, Wickers don't make furnaces. They just buy them. Aye, they did put up yor idea to Ganmore's, them that are the experts in furnaces. Their man was in.'

'And what did he have to say aboot it, Ganmore's man ah mean?' Tom butted in with his eager question.

'He didn't say owt much. Said it was interestin'. That's aal he said. Did they send your drawin's back?'

Did they send his drawings back? Tom had forgotten about them. He shook his head negatively.

'Mek sure you get them back! Things that can't be digested on Monday, some folks might get an appetite for by Friday, if you see what ah mean?'

Tom's head was buzzing. He only had a vague idea what Mister Col meant. He'd had to absorb a lot of disappointments. He wasn't to go into the drawing office; he wasn't going to get his 'trig' so he could be a pilot. And now, his best idea to date had been thrown out; only because the people around him didn't like change. The world didn't look bright and rosy any more. He thanked Mister Col and went back to his job.

PART SEVEN

Essential Work

'It's like this!' Lang Jack observed as they stared across the river towards Dunston. 'Supposin' this was the River Jordan.'

'But it's not!' Tom called out to him. He was sitting along with the other two on the concrete walkway which was part of the pump-house foundations. It was summer and the cold of the concrete was bearable. Had it been winter they'd have been having their 'bait' in the warmth of the mould-drying stove. But it was summer and they were glad to take the fresh air, if the air at that place, on that placid gloomy day, could be described as fresh.

Where he was, Tom could see the rats playing around the outpour from the Elswick sewer, the peculiar smell from it being blended but not quite lost in foundry smells they knew so well. They were far from the River Jordan.

Lang Jack shook his head which was caped with close-cropped ginger hair. 'I was only supposin'.' Lang Jack was tall and thin and wiry, his big feet, encased in big boots, seemed out of place on such a stick-like frame. It was not surprising he had another title, Swan Vestas.

'But how can you suppose that?' Tom asked. He was the direct opposite to Lang Jack; short, powerful, with an abundance of thick wavy hair. Hair like a mat from dirty foundry vapours, if it wasn't washed often. It didn't get washed often. 'We aal know that this is the Tyne and that drain over there, it's the Elswick sewer from aal the Elswick netties. Aye, and them's Elswick rats.'

They were quiet for a while, busy unwrapping newspaper packs that contained the bait. Further conversation was withheld while examination took place.

Philosophy took a back seat as they scanned the content of what mother had packed for their dinner.

'Bloody Spam again!' Danny grumbled. 'I hate Spam! You canna do a day's work on Spam sandwiches.' Danny was midway between the other two. In looks and in disposition. Taller than Tom but shorter than Lang Jack. A nervous type of lad who had to be always on the move. A learning craftsman with a guilt complex of any small error.

'Seems to make you strong enough.' Tom grinned across to Lang Jack who grinned back in understanding. 'Saw you chuck a bad'un well out into the river this mornin', when you thought no-one was lookin'. There's not many fellas can heave a twenty-pound castin' forty yards. It must be that National bread! Tattie peelins' and horsemuck must be good for us.'

Danny's face took on an expression of alarm. 'Col didn't see me, did he?'

'Col? Why, no man! He wouldn't have put on his workin' hat by then. You's always first out on the gantry, Danny.' Tom laughed. Col, the head foreman, was bald as a coot and every morning did a lightning switch to hide his embarrassment.

'Oh aye, but you was out there, Tom? What was you doin' there, out on the gantry? Hopin' to see Betty belly-button?' Lang Jack tittered.

Tom reddened and hung his head. Was that the reason he was out on the gantry so early? He poured out the hot sweet tea from his tea can into the can lid. He balanced that on the mouth of the can, that in the lid being warmed by the liberal supply underneath. He sought to quickly change the subject. That embarrassing subject.

'Aye, Danny'll spoil aal yor plans about the River Jordan and baptism, Swan. He's got that many bad'uns in there, the river bed will be like the Rocky Mountains. Aal the folks would break their toes.'

'Ah wasn't thinkin' 'bout the River Jordan for baptism. Ah was just thinkin', gettin' outa this place, into the Services, it's just like crossin' over to Jordon, if you's see what ah mean? Do you see? We's trapped here in this soddin' reserved occupation, eatin' this 'lastic' Spam, when aal the lads are out there.'

'Feedin' on real eggs and bacon!' Danny cut in. 'Them lucky buggers in the Forces has every bloody thing. Aal the lasses, Betty belly-button wouldn't give you a second look, Tom if one of them Brylcreem boys was around.'

Tom grunted. He'd never give in to that. But that Betty belly-button, she was a very disturbing influence. Just why did she jump up onto the window sole, in the girls' rest-room, and under cover of the frosted glass lift her dress, pull her pants down, and press herself into the window? Did she do it as soon as she saw Tom? Or did anything in trousers take her fancy? Tom liked to think she did it only for him. How many others thought the same? If he was excited by Betty's act, Tom wasn't too sure about Betty; she was too daring. He'd never met Betty and wasn't likely to. The girls working in the little garment factory, perched higher than the foundry, across the main East-West railway, had no way of making personal contact. The two soldiers stationed on the gantry, and the festoon of barbed wire, ensured there'd be no meeting.

'Aye,' Tom chewed on his Spam sandwich and reflected on those Brylcreem boys. Blue uniform, smart cap, tilted at just the right angle, nice clean face. A fella in the forces could have a bath every week, maybe a shower, every day? The picture of that well-washed, clean-cut hero occupied his thoughts. He scowled when he thought of his present surroundings, what the management had said to apprentices who wanted to join up, 'It takes brains to make them, son, any silly bugger can shoot them. Circumstances made you a maker on essential work. Makers are targets! Wear your helmet, son, keep it with you always!'

Where was that steel helmet now? They had gone out of fashion. They'd been carried everywhere for a couple of months. With it and that gas-mask they'd become an adornment surplus to requirements. That R.A.F. cap, now, that was worth wearing. Tom could imagine himself waiting outside that little garment factory on Scotswood Road, with clean R.A.F.-type face, all the lasses giving him the eye, and waiting to meet. Tom still wasn't too sure about Betty belly-button, she was a bit much. Most of the girls at the garment factory would go as far as waving to the apprentices. A few would lift their skirts and flash their thighs, under cover of that frosted glass. But that Betty belly-button, she took your breath away. She was so rude. She was disgusting. This did not prevent the supposed prudish Tom and company from sneaking out onto the gantry whenever they could escape the eagle eye of the dreaded Col. The daring Betty, however, she rationed her appearances.

'She's a Garmin spy, sent to interrupt production!' some wag had quipped.

'What ah really think is, ah think we's in hell!' Swan Vestas made the shattering observation in the time between his next mouthful of American fried dried-egg sandwich.

'Aye, could be. But them in the R.A.F., they's not in hell. They're in heaven. That's where we ought to be, floatin' around up there like the angels.' Tom flicked a piece of his precious Spam down to the rats having a shower in the spume of the sewer.

Swan Vestas continued the theme. 'Ah thinks we's bein' punished for something we did in another time, another life.'

Danny, the most impressionable, stopped his champing on the Spam he hated. 'You mean we wasn't moulders? What was we then? Was we just pattern-makers, or was we, was we just labourers?' The thought appalled him.

Tom chuckled. 'Him up there, he's got his eye on you. Knows aal about them bad'uns you've chucked in the Tyne. You might come back as a pattern-maker.'

'Garn, yor daft!' Danny wasn't happy about that. The dreaded Col was enough on his back. Now, "Him up there", did he really know?

'It's true! Him up there, he's a bigger boss than Col. Him up there, he was the first moulder. The first foundryman. He'll know all what's goin' on down here. Who makes the good'uns and the bad'uns. It says so in the Bible, doesn't it, Swan?' Tom grinned across to his ally.

'Course! God was the first moulder. Col says so. He melted the metal that made us aal.' Swan waved in agreement.

'We's not made of metal!' Danny now knew they were pulling his leg.

'Not made of metal? Aye, maybe not. Not iron or bronze, but a sort'a metal. Didn't that fella say, us had our metal brayed out?' Swan looked across to his ally. 'That means we's buggered!'

'What fella? He must be crackers! We's made of flesh and blood.' Danny guessed his mates were at the usual ploy of pulling his leg. But sometimes, he was innocently believing.

'Course we is, now! But when you was first made, yor Dad poured his metal into yor Ma. Just like we pour metal into the moulds we make.' Swan had it all worked out.

Danny's jaw sagged. The champing on that hated Spam stopped, his mouth still open in sudden thought. He decided he didn't like Swan's theory.

'Hey you, Swan, you be careful what you say about my Ma!' Danny's hackles had risen. No-one was going to talk like that about his Ma. 'My Ma doesn't do things like that!'

Tom hastened to straighten out the matter. Danny was an

introvert who could act in a physical fashion should he be taken too far. Young strong apprentice moulders had tough hands and arms. If Tom could match Danny, he still shrank from the thought.

'Swan didn't mean just yor Ma, Danny! He meant everybody's Ma. His and mine as well. All life starts with somebody pouring metal into a mould. Your Ma is a mould just like all Ma's. Aye, and them lasses up there, over the line, they's all moulds ready for fillin'.'

Swan had to take the opportunity offered. He cut in quick. 'That's why that Betty belly-button is always flashin' her runner-box to Tom, here!'

'She's not! She's not!' Tom hotly exclaimed. 'She doesn't do it for me.'

The pressure was now lifted from Danny and he took advantage. 'Hey, if it wasn't for the line and the barbed wire and them two soldiers, she'd be ower here hot as, he-he-he, you know what!'

Tom glowered. he'd have liked to believe it was true. That Betty did her stuff only for him. But he knew Betty's act could be seen by anybody who cared to watch. He changed the subject. 'What do you think about the dredger comin'? You remember, Col said it at last Monday's inspection?'

'Never mind changin' the subject! Look, Swan, he's blushin'?' Danny kept the spotlight on the hapless Tom.

'Aye, so he is! But so was you, Danny! You knew what Col was hintin' when he said the dredger was comin'.' Swan's jaws champed on in rhythm with his speech. If you had the misfortune to be in front of him, you'd be showered with a sputter of fried Spam and bread, the thin grass beneath their dangling legs having the benefit. The pump-house foundation was like a quay except that it was never touched by the river. Perhaps a most unusual spring tide might have brought the River Tyne lapping right up to the trio's boots. Swan's in particular.

'Aye, the dredger's comin', Dan! It'll operate right there.' Tom seized the initiative. Anything to dim the image of the dreaded Betty. He pointed along past Danny's and Swan's legs to a position overlooked by the gantry; Danny's favourite sacrificial spot to the river god.

All three were caught up in the thought of the guilt that accompanied that Monday morning inspection. It was the weekly routine criticism for the apprentices, headed by the dreaded Col.

Any casting that had failed to pass the primary inspection was laid out in a special spot on the fettling floor and each had to bear the scornful insinuations of the head foreman. The particular guilty apprentice would squirm and sweat wondering if Col would be in a bad mood that particular Monday.

It went something like this …

'Aye now … who's is this work of art?' He would already know the culprit, but you had to stand forward in full view of the grinning mature craftsmen.

'Oh, it's yors, Jack, (Swan Vestas). Do you think the Admiral would like to buy that? Would you want to send yor lad down in a submarine with that scrapper?'

Col's head would nod like a donkey, encouraging the lad to speak. It was best not to speak; but personal pride needed protection.

'Oh I see! The metal was too hot? Was it? I must get my glasses changed, I could swear that was cross-jointed! Aye, cross-jointed, a cardinal sin seeing you's got moulding boxes with "he" halfs and "she" halfs. You know what that's aal about, don't you? You know where what goes where, don't you? Did you see the river police pull that poor lass outa the river the other day? Did you see she was floatin' face up? Do you know why?'

Swan Vestas had shook his head in bewilderment.

'Aye, well, next time you see the police pullin' a man outa the river, you'll see that the man will be floatin', face down. Are you with me? Face up for lasses and face down for fellas. Maybe that'll help you to remember what goes where next time you make that job.'

They didn't know whether Col was pulling their leg or not. Nevertheless, it was gruesome hints like that kept the apprentices on their toes.

The others got their share of the homespun philosophy.

'And you, Thomas, what's this mess? Oh, you think it was cast short? The pourer missed your runner-box?' Tom vainly tried to explain what had gone wrong, in his opinion.

'Would you like to buy it, boy? That's the crunch, will anybody buy it? Do you know how much it costs to melt metal? Next time, boy, a bigger better cleaner runner-box. One that won't waste that expensive molten metal. Aye, and make sure the bugger's not been used before!'

There were sheepish grins at that. They were beginning to get the point.

It was Bill Wilson's turn next. He stood forward in humble mood. He was older than the other three, up for the 'high jump'.

'Aye, you Bill, now don't tell me, this is supposed to be a shell-support casing? Have they changed the design overnight? It wasn't that shape last week. Do you think you should be paid for that? What, the 'cramper' put the cramps on too tight? Well, lad, you know the answer to that. Yor the craftsman, yor the one responsible!'

Bill stepped back suitably subdued.

Danny was hovering. he had no work up for criticism. He was sticking his neb in; perhaps he had a guilty conscience? He wasn't prone to bragging, he worried too much for that. He shouldn't have been there. If Col hadn't seen him, he might not have triggered off Col's unfailing memory. Col gave a grin and a nod to Danny.

'Aye, there yar Dan. No scrappers from you last week? Aye, aye, you're a credit to the craft, son. Keep up the good work, lad.' Mr. Col gave another little grin. 'Y'know what they say's about fellas that makes nee bad'uns? They say the buggers does nee work.'

Those who had squirmed under the critical rhetoric of Mr. Col had their pain eased by his next remarks. After all, they just couldn't bring themselves to complain, 'Hey, he chucks all his bad'uns in the Tyne.'

Col waved an accusing finger at them all. ' Mind you, lads, the dredger will be comin' next week. It'll be makin' its way up to us. Mind now, ah want no complaints from the crew! Whoever has that air-pistol, you keep it for the rats. Ah want no lad of mine swimmin' over to the dredger and paintin' Garmin crosses and swastikas on it, and using those as an excuse for target practice.' Mr. Col gazed at Danny. 'It'll be interestin' to see what the dredger picks up. We might get some free scrap? Eh? What say, lads?' Mr. Col waved them away back to their work. A very sudden bowel movement caused top craftsman Danny to dart away to the easing station not very far from his usual pitching position.

Mr. Col said nothing about those little balloons that came out of the sewer. Those were the usual targets for the air-pistol gunners. They'd blow them up, tie and weight them, then throw them out into the river. He who burst most was the champion. Tom did wonder why Monday was the best time for those balloons.

The three philosophers, seated on the pump-house footway, now filled with a mash of Spam and American dried-egg sandwiches, mixed with liberal quantities of hot sweet tea, drooped in drowsy repose to those full stomachs. The tea, made from a thick stiff paste of tea leaves, plus sugar, plus condensed milk, drenched and drowned in boiling water, presented a neutral base for that American aid. It was in this condition that our three articled hell-bound prisoners received their baptism. Not the baptism Swan Vestas had in mind.

He might have been dreaming of John-the-Baptist. He drifted back to reality and murmured, 'Aah thought aah could hear the first buzzer?' He focused on the power station directly opposite. On those four tall chimneys. They dissolved into four tall, grey threatening men. They lost out to that full belly.

The dredger occupied Danny's thoughts. Would its buckets betray him. Would the eagle-eyed scanners on the screens miss Danny's sacrificial iron in among the Tyne's muddy dross?

Tom, he was up in the clouds at the controls of his Spitfire. That magic deadly button operating those eight machine-guns was close to his thumb. He was about to press it and blow that enemy aircraft right out of the sky, when, that well-known voice said ... 'C'mon lad, you's got another half-hour. Time to make another one, for the boys out there, anybody can shoot them, it takes a craftsman to make them!' And there was that awful Betty belly-button. Tom dreamily wondered if he dared slip out to the gantry, just to take a peep?

The first buzzer always sounded five minutes before the proper starting time. It came to arouse you from your dreaming. It hadn't sounded! But something inherent in Swan had warned him of something ...

Tom's thoughts drifted up again. How did you get out of this hell-hole and get into the seat of that Spitfire? He recalled the recent conversations down at the recruiting office in Grainger Street.

'Aye lads, the army wants men! Strappin' lads just like you. Tell you what, go back to Wickers, tell the management we wants you, ask for your release, written permission, mind, then we'll have you fightin' Garmins in six weeks.' It was a well-rehearsed speech the recruiting sergeant had used many times before. He knew there'd be no release. Not for these lads. It didn't help to say so. Better to extend a little hope, that one day, maybe? Tom's thoughts drifted on, a lazy grin crept across his face, would Betty be doin' her act this afternoon? ...

Essential Targets

The lone raider, sleek and shark-like, clothed in most sombre colour, almost funereal in appearance, with the dreaded iron-cross markings, raced on its special mission.

Night bombing had been an irregular occurrence in the Tyne district and with some limited success. Tom and company could testify to that. If vital targets were missed, the nightly terror brought to the district remained. To alert the radar was all that was necessary to put the whole district out of its bed. Sleepless nights took their toll on the working population. If you couldn't hit the vital targets, there were other ways of grinding people down.

The foundry had been hit twice with fire bombs; metallic alloy devices not unlike flying fish. Every apprentice had a dud incendiary bomb, or the remains of one. They'd been told to hand them in. They did! One for them to brag about, and another for the dreaded Col. They thought how silly it all was. Trying to set fire to hell with matches. That's how they saw the foundry in their present mood.

Finding vital targets embracing the winding misty Tyne district was very much a hit and miss affair, a lottery no-one wished to win. The River Tyne resembled a drunken snake when viewed from the air even in the best light. The lone raider from Luftflotte 3, from a station in Belgium, was on yet another innovative run.

The pilot's instructions, 'Find the gate through the low-level radar at Whitby, North Yorkshire, fly West over the moors then head North. Pick up the signal from the 40,000 volt main grid, follow it to the power station at Dunston on Tyne, there you will find four targets! (1) the Dunston power station, (2) the main power line and pylon which feeds the Wickers plant, (3) the foundry making naval work, (4) the main rail link between East and West!

Tom and company never knew how important they were, outside their own district.

It was Dunston Hill that appeared to cause the problem. Or was it the gunner's scream through the intercom.

'Achtung Spitfire!' It was not. It could not have been because the Messerschmitt Me 262a didn't have that rear gunner to watch and shoot any pursuer. It had a crew of one, the pilot, Feldwebel Fritz Werner, who had the task of knocking out the chosen strategic target, the Wickers armaments factory. Two bombs wouldn't destroy the factory; but they could destroy the power supply.

The Me 262a had its range stretched to the limit with the addition of drop tanks. It had enough fuel to get to its target and back to its base. Just enough. The pilot had the knowledge that his aircraft was 'state-of-the-art', and with its tops speed of 541 m.p.h., it could outrun any allied aircraft.

It was the very first jet aircraft to fly and was still experimental. He knew that as a stable gun and bomb platform the Me 262a had yet to be proven. Twin jet aircraft at top speed had a nasty reputation of snaking, and at the wrong time. This was going to be an ultra-fast shallow dive-bomb attack. The method most likely to succeed.

Feldwebel Werner knew he'd be detected by the air defence. He also knew his speed was such he'd be difficult to intercept. Nothing except the worst of bad luck could prevent Werner from getting to his target.

He'd followed the high-tension buzz beneath him and all he wanted now was to view those four tall chimneys of the power station. His hand had already sought the bomb release as he waited for the tall chimneys to appear in the reflex sight ahead of him at eye-level on his windshield. He'd already dropped his extra tanks when he approached the coast at Whitby. When he let go his two bombs, he'd be able to touch his fastest speed. He'd be away before the R.A.F. could lay a glove on him.

He was wrong! The Hurricane from Ouston was on him before he got to the power station. They knew what he was after. Werner almost felt the blast of those eight guns. But it was long range shooting; almost in desperation. Werner's heart skipped a beat. He had to get rid of those bombs to give him top speed. If there was one R.A.F. plane, there'd be others, gathering for the kill!

He automatically checked his compass, speed indicator and artificial horizon. His left hand sought the comfort of the loading button on his four 30mm. Rheinmetall cannon; fire-power superior to his enemy, but not much use if you were the quarry. If only those four guns would shoot rearwards ...

He'd be back home in just over an hour, if nothing went wrong.

The Whickham-Dunston hill came up at 500 m.p.h. Over the hill were those four tall chimneys. He felt the breath of that hungry hound on the back of his neck. The target appeared in his sight and with only his left hand on the control column, he pulled the bomb release lever. The Me 262a bounded forward like a racehorse out of the starting stalls. Feldwebel Fritz Werner was up and away before his bombs struck.

Essential Killing

Was it the snaking problem of jet aircraft that saved our three dozing apprentices? Had the aircraft not veered slightly to port as it did, Feldwebel Fritz Werner would have earned his Iron Cross. Still, he did stop production of army and navy socks, in Betty belly-button's factory?

'You lads hurry along to yor shelter! Never mind if it's not the one you've been allocated. Any bugger will do! Get movin', there might be more of them buggers buzzin' around!' The mature craftsmen hurried the lads to the shelters, after the initial insanity of that lightning attack had dulled. All that Tom and company had heard was the screaming of the jet aircraft and the rattle of the machine-guns of the pursuing Hurricane. They'd been well shielded from the bomb blasts by the pump-house and the main foundry building above them. The air-raid sirens finally sounded, minutes after the attacker had gone.

Those inside the main factory building poured out to their appointed shelter. There they would sit till the all-clear sounded. Those with special duties would stay, checking machinery, damping down furnaces. If metal was ready to be tapped from a cupola, it had to be tapped. Those already in the shelters thanked their lucky stars they didn't have to operate ladles full of molten iron or bronze. Being bombed was bad enough. To be burned to the bone with that fiery liquid, that was a fate only for the most unfortunate.

Col, the dreaded gaffer, was there directing operations. Only when he was certain that everyone had left the foundry would he leave himself. He would take up his .22 target rifle he now kept in his office. He was in the Home Guard and that gave him some credence as to guardianship. With his weapon hefted on his shoulder he would march to his shelter. Stationing himself at the doorway and ignoring the pleas of the 'official' shelter warden, him with the arm-band, Col would scan the skies for other raiders. Exactly what he could do with that puny weapon, the sniggerings from the gloom of the shelter wanted to know. Col would mutter, 'Well, you never know. There are such things as paratroops.' To back this theory, he would touch his nose, sagely. But only to the mature craftsmen.

'You know what goes on up there, in that little place? The place where yor money changes colour?' He referred to the small research foundry attached to the main foundry. 'Them Garmin buggers would like to know aal about that high duty light alloy. That's why them two soldiers is always on guard!'

From the doorway Col would reign supreme. Nobody could escape his theories. A nuisance at that time to imprisoned apprentices; later discovered as a fountain of practical knowledge. Col was a 'royal'. He'd never make top management. But management couldn't survive without his like. He never tired of telling the apprentices the importance of being a craftsman.

'God was the first fella to melt things, just like us. Do you know that, lads? God was the first moulder.'

'Was God a fella?' a voice from the gloom would ask.

'Course he was!' Col would enjoy the banter. 'Doesn't it say in the Bible that God made man in his own image?'

'How would God do that?' A titter from the gloom. 'Did he use his-sel as a pattern?'

Swan Vestas nudged Tom and chanced his arm in the gloomy shelter. 'How did God know what he looked like, Mr. Col? There was nee mirrors in them days. We aal know every moulder needs a pattern to work from. Maybe God was a pattern-maker, before he was a moulder?'

That was sure to arouse Mr. Col. He was always having rows with pattern-makers. He considered them to be inferior to moulders.

'They's only carpenters with contraction rules, son. We's the real brains in the foundry. The end product rests with us!'

The red-headed glow tried again.

'Wasn't Jesus a carpenter, Mr. Col?' That was a difficult one.

'Aye, aye, so they say.' There was a pause. 'Aye, but he was the Son of God, not as high as God. Just an apprentice like yor-sel, Jack. You couldn't expect God to make anybody as perfect as his-sel, now could you? We aal know that nee castin' is as perfect as its pattern. There is always some loss of definition. Just take a look in a mirror, Jack lad. God must have made a few scrappers in his time, just like you, son!'

Swan's red face was shielded by the gloom. That was a putdown. It was always risky trying to take a rise out of Mr. Col. He could knock you down, and pick you up.

'Of course, lad, the "swan" is one of God's more graceful creatures. And after aal, son, God tried to make you in his image. Maybe you was made on Monday, or Friday; tapering-down day.'

Somebody had to challenge that.

'Saturday was God's tapering-down day. He rested on Sunday!'

Some other thinker had a thought.

'The bugger had a better job than us. We work all bloody week long! Moulders is only labourers with a few brains.' That must have been a pattern-maker.

'You see, lads,' Mr. Col pressed on. 'There's really only two sorts of people. There's them that work, and them that watch. Take Cain and Abel for example. Abel was a lazy bugger who watched his brother dee aal the work. Cain, he was a moulder just like us. He got tired of deein' aal the work, and gave his brother his cards. Course, the way they tells it in the Bible, Cain cast a sword in the sand and knocked his brother off. Just like we's doin' to the Garmins! They was real cruel buggers in them days, always choppin' off some poor bugger's hand for next to nowt. As for swords, the swords we makes these days, they's got wings on! We's more advanced these days. These days, we does aal our killin' at long distance, just like that bugger that just killed them lasses, up there, over the line.'

It was the first the apprentices had heard about the death of Betty and her workmates. Even then, they hardly took it in.

They didn't weep when it finally sunk in about the death of Betty and her mates. Tough lads like these couldn't be seen weeping. When the got burned by splashes of molten iron, they were allowed to jump and curse. But not weep. Weeping was taboo!

The flattened factory was all that remained of the seductive Betty. The little room with the frosted glass, where she did her provocative act, was no more. It was as if it had never been. It was beyond their understanding. You just didn't do things like that! Despite the sly grins and nudges that accompanied the latest rude remark about Betty, you just didn't drop bombs on girls. Not on lasses, that wasn't fair. Lasses were lamps that brightened the dark days. Hell to them who put that lamp out!

There was a general move to the recruiting offices the next day. When the shock of the bombing turned to hatred they all went down to the office in Grainger Street. All ten of them.

'What the devil is the matter with your lads?' the recruiting sergeant demanded of the management over the telephone. 'They won't go away!'

They did eventually go home; not back to the factory. They didn't want to be reminded of Betty and those battered remains. Some came back next day. The others drifted back and got on with the job. Suggestions that output was the best way of striking back fell on deaf ears. There really was nothing better than shooting the sods down by yourself!

The sage craftsmen took the youngsters aside and told them the old story. They told them how important they were. It was the same as before, 'Any fool can shoot them, but it takes brains and skill to make them. You can help kill more of the buggers by doin' what yor trained to do!'

It was probably Ginger Craggs and John Walton who broke open the cage. There was one positive way of getting slung out of your reserved occupation and your indentures cancelled. Perhaps it was Ginger's protracted failure to get out of the foundry and into the Services that was the cause of their extreme action.

Johnny, an extremely neat worker, had produced his daily quota of small gun-mounting moulds. There they were, fifteen open moulds perfect in every detail, waiting for their filling. Ginger appeared and walked over each one carefully and deliberately. Johnny, it is said in retaliation, did the same act to Ginger's moulds. Pandemonium.

Mr. Col sent for the apprentice training officer, Captain Finn. He requested the presence of the works doctor; had the lads gone round the bend? Was it sabotage? You could get shot for sabotage! So it was rumoured.

They were both suspended and out on the street. In an hour they were at the R.A.F. recruiting office. They were in! They'd volunteered as air-gunners. There were plenty of vacancies for air-gunners but not a lot of candidates.

In six weeks they were back at the foundry on a week's leave. The others looked and felt dingy and shabby beside those two R.A.F. shining heros of the Brylcreem hair and the cheeky cap. All was forgiven. They'd be allowed to finish their apprenticeship when they came back from the war.

Ginger and Johnny flashed their chevron-bedecked sleeves for all they were worth. If only Betty and the other girls had been there to see. They were officers in all but the commission, and in only six weeks; such was the need of the war machine.

Col was beaming, just like the others. After all, they were his lads. He'd helped to train them. His beam was dipped to a frown, soon as they left.

'They's shootin' the poor buggers down over Garminy ten a penny! Weapons designed way back in the dark ages is nee good against the cannon the Jerry night-fighters has. Let's just pray the lads gets the first one in! That's the one that counts ... the first one!'

They were dead in a week. Their very first raid over Germany. The notorious telegram read, 'Missing, presumed dead!' The 'presumed dead' said it all. No chance! Had they run into Feldwebel Fritz and his four 30mm. cannon? The little union flags grew like mushrooms on his Me 262a. Those four cannon could overreach the .303 Brownings in the big bombers. One short burst of three rounds from each gun at 1000 yards could cut both the tail gunner and the midships gunner to bits. The braking effect of the gunners and their armour prevented the shells reaching right through to the pilot and navigator. The six-gun sting in the tail of the big bomber gone, it was left dead or dying. Easy meat. The next burst at shorter range gave the coup-de-grâce. Like Col had said, 'Get the first one in, that's the one that counts!'

Despite the death and destruction of the times, it was terrible news. It hurt worse than the death of Betty. They'd never touched her, remote in her frosted glass.

They'd all played foota and cricket together out on the gantry. Games often interrupted by Betty's antics. It began to feel as if everybody was going to some other place. Was it loneliness or thoughts of revenge that now occupied their thoughts?

Tom, Danny and Swan Vestas had grown strangely quiet. Work was far from their minds.

Essential Revenge

'C'mon now then, lads. No dawdlin'. Let's get on with it!' It was the foreman, not the dreaded Col. 'Have you seen my specs, lads? Ah just had them a few minutes ago.'

'Here you are, Mr. Bell.' Tom reached over to the foreman and swung the elusive specs, swinging from the foreman's ear, back on to both ears. Mr. Bell, 'Bellie', invariably lost his specs to one ear.

'Oh, aye! Thanks, lad!' Off he went, bent on his duty.

Swan Vestas pointed to him as he went. 'Just look at him. He's got that much on his mind, the poor man doesn't know where he's at. Nobody in their right mind would be a foreman in a foundry. It's an ulcer job for sure.'

'That's us in twenty years from now!' Danny looked at the other two, quizzically. They got his drift.

'What do you say, Swan?' Tom looked up at the towering Swan.

'Aye, let's go!' Swan led the way.

'Yes lads, yes we want bright young fellows, just like you; if you can pass the medical.' The recruiting officer gave the three a keen but weary scanning. If he had any idea that these youngsters would never come back home again, he gave no sign. It was his duty to get them in. The 'No Vacancy' sign to those on essential work had been removed. If you fancied your chances against the night-fighters in the air battle over Germany, you were in. You had at least to be able to fit into the power turrets.

The officer walked the few steps in front of the three lined up, tallest on the left. They stood as smartly as craftsman could, still in possession of the sweat and grime from their work, the quick wash they'd had hardly making any difference. It was as if they were looking, if not at God, at one of his disciples at least. They were fascinated by that R.A.F. blue uniform. They felt distinctly dirty and shabby in his presence. He had his orders! 'You can have only one! You choose which one!'

He stopped in front of Swan; gave him the twice-over. Looked down at those big feet.

'Sorry, laddie. You'll never fit into a power turret. So that leaves you out. Sorry, laddie.'

He moved to Danny, next in line. Danny was trying hard to restrain his excitement. His hands clenched and unclenched under that R.A.F. gaze. The officer knew the signs. Danny was a finely tuned craftsman. It didn't take much to upset Danny.

'We can take only one of you. So it's between you two.' He gave Tom the benefit of that steady scrutiny. Tom was the right size. He would fit easily into that turret. Get out quickly too, if he had need. It had to be stocky, serene Tom. He didn't want to be an air-gunner; he wanted to be a pilot, the engine driver.

'You the one with the air-pistol?' The man in blue was facing Tom.

'Eh? Who me, sir?' Tom was surprised. Who had been talking?

'They tell me you're a good shot?'

'That's him, sir!' Swan nodded, grinning. 'He's the best rat-shooter in Wickers. He's the one.'

The smart blue uniform absorbed that willingly.

'Alright, lads, this is the way it's going to be. It's between you two. As there's nothing to choose between you – one's as good as the other – we'll toss for it.' He put his hand in his pocket and searched around. He brought out a penny. His special penny.

They were gathered around to hear Tom's letter read out. He'd been back to see them all, his sergeant's stripes standing out like brilliant spearheads. He was cleaner now than he had ever been, his six weeks' training bringing him to a peak he'd not known before. He was no longer a maker, he was a destroyer. Or would he be destroyed? They all wondered if that visit would be the last they'd see of him.

Swan read out the letter.

> Thanks to everyone for all the good wishes and the food parcels. Please don't send any more food. Keep it for yourselves. There's plenty of grub here. All the chocolate you want. Plenty meat. All sorts of jam with real white bread. You only get real eggs and bacon when you fly. I'll bc flying every night, unless. Tell Mr. Col not

to worry, my arms are longer than Ginger and Johnny's. Tell him I'll meet him in Halifax on my next leave. Remember, I am the French-letter champion and who knows, I just might meet up with that Jerry one dark night, that sod who put poor Betty down.

Best wishes to all. See you on my leave.

Tom

'What's he mean, Mr. Col?' they asked the fountain of knowledge. 'Tom's never been to Halifax?'

'He means he's in a Halifax bomber, son. He means he's got a tail turret and two big guns. Guns that will reach out further than Ginger and Johnny's. It means he just might be able to get the first one in! The one that counts. He'll be back to see us. The French-letter champion!' Mr. Col hid a tear. Moulders don't cry.

They were flighting in like vultures coming home to roost. Great sombre four-engined destructive devices with empty bellies. Their tired crews glad to return to life. They would live another day, at least.

The pilot and crew of the Halifax with the code sign BeeBee 09 had been last to land, priority given to their colleagues with wounded aboard. They watched helplessly as one aircraft crashed while landing. There was no fire, as the long journey had drained the fuel tanks. An ordinary crash-landing; that was a bonus.

Their ground crew rushed to meet them. Wounded knights to be carried off to the surgeon? The crew could feel those eyes as they scanned the body of the aircraft looking for the signs of damage. There was none! Somebody wouldn't have to work all day and all night.

With engines stopped, the crew relaxed in their seats, each thanking whatever God he prayed to for safe return. Their duty was done, for the time being. There was only one duty these days; blast the retreating enemy till he surrendered. He had a mighty tough hide.

Stiff bodies, cold and resistive, were forced out of seats. There was no hurry now. On the tarmac they assembled with quiet nods of agreement and relief. They were glad to be back home. They watched while ambulances raced to other aircraft. Almost instinctively they all glanced to the tail of BeeBee 09. They made their way there, rubbing limbs into better life.

The skipper looked up to the tail turret.

'You there, Geordie?' he called out. The turret was unmarked.

'Aye, I'm here, skipper, and my name's Tom, not Geordie!'

They all laughed at that. All North country men had to be called Geordie. They didn't know why.

'You O.K., Tom? C'mon out. You're not wounded, are you?'

'Naa, just cold. Too damn cold. Too stiff to move. I'll be alright, skipper.'

'How do you do it? That's six you've put down. You must have eyes like a cat.' They all knew that any of those six fighters shot down over Germany could have ended their lives.

'Ah was, French-letter champion, back home,' came the answer. They laughed at that. It must be one of those funny North country jokes that only Northerners understood.

PART EIGHT

On being Earnest

It was not the sort of day for sitting outside on the gantry or on the pump-house walkway. It was a day for propping yourself up against the warm walls of the mould-drying stove and digging into your fried-egg sandwiches.

Those four tall chimneys of the Dunston power station still menaced their outdoor debating platform. A reminder of the day that Garmin raider with four cannon in its nose flashed over the river at them. It was rain that had driven them indoors; not an uncommon occurrence in North-east England.

The war was over, that is to say, the fighting, the physical conflict had ended. The long job of picking up the pieces had begun. American dried egg was now being slowly replaced by real egg sandwiches.

Tom had come home from the war. He'd come to finish his apprenticeship. All apprentices, forced into uniform or those volunteering, all were allowed to finish that apprenticeship. It was most important that you received the document that recorded the fact that you had satisfactorily completed your time.

He hadn't done much work that morning. Col and others had fussed around, glad to see him back. Indeed he was a menace to production; everybody wanted to have a word.

Mr. Col was in favour of him eating his bait in the office.

It was something like his first day at Wickers, when Fred the millwright had taken him in hand. Here he was sitting in these strange new overalls in this dirty gloomy place in earshot of rumbling overhead cranes.

So as not to upset the great man, Tom spent half the dinner-hour with him and then went out to join the gang. He knew where to find them on that rainy day, as he left the office with Col's advice still ringing in his ears.

'Just take it easy, Tom. Take it step by step. You'll maybe find it hard to get back in yor stride after that toff's time you've had in the R.A.F.'

Tom's smile shielded a grimace. A toff's time? A posh uniform perhaps, but he wasn't sure about having a posh time in the R.A.F.. They didn't know it, but he was glad to be back in the dirty-noisy-quiet of the foundry; this place of honest sanity.

This aura of glamour of the uniformed hero which now proceeded, was only in the minds of his mates; Tom felt anything but heroic. As Col had indicated, the adulation wouldn't last; he would become an ordinary man because he'd be doing ordinary work.

'It's a man's work that determines the man! Yor a craftsman. God was the best craftsman. Nee mere man'll be that good. Remember, son, killin' six Garmins was yor duty at that time, you might have thought you was God, up there, dealin' justice? But now you're on the ground, like us mere mortals.' It was said with kindness and sincerity. To help rather than hinder. Did Col already know his thoughts? His mental tribulations?

Would the people around him ever guess he was only the shell of the boy who went to war? The major-domo had noticed; she was glad to have him back in any condition.

Before leaving for service in the R.A.F., Tom had been a stocky, slightly overweight, long-haired, level-tempered youth. Now he was a taller, thinner youth-man with a belly that wouldn't hold up his trousers.

'They must have been starvin' the poor lad!' Granny Bella complained. 'He'll need good thick broth and suet puddin's to fill him oot.'

'It's aal them carrots they fed us, Gran,' he'd joked to the old lady. 'Carrots counteract the poison in the system, make yor reactions quicker.'

'You means they move yor bowels. Aye, that's a good thing if carrots move yor bowel. What you really wants is sulphur and treacle. That black stuff is best. Aye, sulphur and black treacle, that's the stuff for coolin' young lad's blood doon.' She sat there as always with fat hands clasped, spouting her wealth of practical experience. 'Raw carrots is only for gallawas, not for folks.'

'Did you ever see a gallawa or a rabbit wearin' specs Gran? Gallawas and rabbits can see in the dark. That's why they feed air-crew in the R.A.F. on carrots every day, so we can see in the dark.' It was a jocular remark that left the old lady silent. Then she said, 'Fancy that!' She then turned to Nobbler to ask for confirmation, when she saw him grinning at Tom. She didn't ask Nobbler if he'd ever seen a rabbit or a gallawa with glasses.

'Cheeky tinker!' she snapped, but really liking the repartee. Tombo could do no wrong these days.

She then smiled, a crafty sort of smile. 'You'll be gettin' yor-sel a lass, now that you's done with the sarvices?' She was a great one for pairing young people off. If everybody was paired off proper, the world would be a far better place, in her view. Obviously most of her predictions were based on the value of the family's store book. Did she have somebody in mind for Tom?

The major-domo came to his rescue, protective as ever. To reinforce her words she got up from her seat. She blocked off Tom from his Gran.

'Plenty of time for that sort of thing, after he's finished his time.' Was it a gentle hint that she, and only she, would be the guardian, the mentor, in that field?

'Aye, that's reet!' Another came to his aid. 'Let the lad be. There's plenty time for him, he'll find his own way.' The ageing Nobbler wasn't grinning now.

He found them where he knew they would be, in the mould-drying stove, the huge mould-carrying bogey hungrily awaiting its daily quota of wet moulds and partially blocking the light to the bait-time tenants.

There they were, their favourite piece of wood for a backrest and an old sack for a seat. The walls and floor of the stove would still be too hot for prolonged contact, hence the protection. Protection against heat or cold to the nether regions was a well-practised religion. If you sat, wherever you sat, it was a long-established custom to protect your rear-end. All young lads would receive the same dire warning, 'Divvent sit on that cold piece of metal, son. Always have yor-sel a piece of wood or you'll get piles. Nowt is as bad as piles.'

There were grunts and grins of welcome when they saw him. He observed Danny, Lang Jack, Perc and Bill Wilson in the gloom. The philosopher wasn't present; he never sat and ate with the plebs. It was a mystery where he got to at bait time. Some said he never stopped for bait but just kept on working.

Tom enjoyed the warmth of the stove but not for long. He enjoyed the polite banter. Polite because as yet they'd not penetrated the hero-worshiping veneer with which he'd been coated. His next act showed how ordinary he was.

'Y'bugger, it's hot in here, wish ah had a seat as hot as this when ah was in the R.A.F.' He went from the stove to get himself a protective slat. He re-entered and after rubbing that hot spot, again took his seat.

'Was it cad up there, up there, when you was a rear-gunner?' The question was asked tentatively. A trial run for an avalanche of other questions. They all wanted to know from he who had been there, this man who had been to hell and had come back again.

Tom grinned and found a more comfortable spot; he could feel the warmth of the floor warming the soles of his feet. It was to him a grand feeling of welcome as the warmth stole away his inhibitions.

'Was it cad up there? Ah'll say it was! It was ...'

'Cad enough to freeze the knackers on a brass monkey?' Perc offered laughingly. The others joined in dutifully, their usual belly-laugh dimmed in the hero's presence.

'Aye, Perc, as cad as that. Aye and colder. Coldest time ah've ever had. It was like ...' He stopped as he searched for the right words. it was hard to describe to these fellows how he really felt. The warmth of the stove brought stimulation.

'Up there, it was so cold, it was as if you were the only man in the world. That's what the cad does to you. They warned us about it. What the cad does to yor brain. Yor brain ceases to function when it's too cad. Y'know, Col was right when he said God was the first moulder, the first foundryman!'

'Huh, he thinks he's God, Col, ah mean,' Danny growled.

'He was right about God bein' a foundryman,' Tom insisted. 'God, or anybody in their right mind, would never do any real plannin' up there in the cold. Naa, God knew he needed warm hands before he could get started to build the world.'

'Aye, warm hands, warm feet and a warm arse, that's what's needed before a fella is comfortable,' agreed Perc.

'Aye, God knew what he was doin'. The first thing he did was to light up the furnace of life, the sun,' Lang Jack chimed in.

Bill Wilson showed signs of impatience. He moved testily in his seat. 'Ah, shut up, you two. Ah want to hear about the war. Ah want to hear how Tom shot down them buggers that murdered poor Betty and her mates. You gave them hell, eh, Tom? What was it really like, blowin' them buggers right out of the sky. Six of the buggers, wasn't it?'

Bill Wilson was one of the apprentices who had given up

trying to get out of the foundry. His visits to the recruiting office had been as unsuccessful as the others. He considered Tom to be highly privileged.

If Tom had felt highly privileged when he went off to war, that was an advantage, with hindsight, he'd give to any of the others.

'Aye, tell us, Tom, what was it really like. What does Garmins look like? Are they all big and fat like them pork butchers?' Danny asked it eagerly.

'Don't be daft, man! Garmins looks just like us, don't they, Tom?' Lang Jack looked down on Danny in disdain. Lang Jack had finished all his night-school classes. He was a mine of information.

'What does Garmins look like? Ah've no idea. Ah never saw one Garmin,' Tom said, staring at the dust-covered floor. 'Except, maybe them two fellas that was diggin' in Reedheugh Hall some years back, they was supposed to be Garmins.' He grimaced as the memories returned. 'Ah wonder if them two really were Garmin spies?'

'Course they was!' Lang Jack interjected. 'The Garmins is very thorough in their plannin'. How do you think that bomber knew exactly where to aim at, that time we was sittin' out by the pump-house?'

It seemed incredible. Was it true? What was it the children called them? Feedle Dee and Feedle Dumb? But not so dumb or daft after all?

'Never mind about them. Nee good cryin' ower spilt milk. What was it like up there, Tom, shootin' them buggers down?' Bill insisted. Insisted on knowing what he had missed.

'What was it like? Nowt to it really. You puts yor uniform on in the mornin'. Puts yor flyin' suit on over yor uniform. You gets a ride out to yor aircraft. You gets in to yor rear turret. You plugs in yor lines ...'

'What lines?' Bill interrupted, living the entire process.

'Yor intercom, yor oxygen. You can't fly to that height

without oxygen. So there you are, all tucked up in a little cold box lookin' back out on to nowt. It was bit like sittin' out by the pump-house on a cold day lookin' at them four tall chimneys. Ah had two tall chimneys instead.'

'Them'd be yor two twenty-mili cannons?' Bill asked eagerly.

'Aye, that's right, Bill. Ah had a better chance than Ginger and Johnny. They only had ordinary .303 guns.'

'And is it right about the carrots? Did they feed you on lots of carrots so you could see in the dark?' These were important questions that needed answers.

Tom rocked back on his seat. The old carrot tale again.

'Course not, you balm pot! Carrots might be good for you but they don't make you see in the dark. Whey no, man. Ah couldn't see a thing when ah was up there.'

'Well, how did you see to hit them Garmin fighters? Hey, yor not startin' to tell us it never happened?' Dismay started to form in Bill's mind. Was their local hero going to turn out to be just a War Office public relations exercise. A ploy to convince young fellas that they wouldn't all be shot to bits?

Gloom descended on the mould-drying stove debaters. Was their link with fame to be lost? Were they to sink back into the commonplace. They'd soared up to the sun on hearing about Tom's decoration. Now, was it all just a myth? Anyway, Tom was, after all, just an ordinary apprentice, just like them; and just like them, ordinary.

'How did ah hit them six night-fighters? Ah told the skipper, when he asked the same question, it was because ah was the French-letter champion of Wickers. He and the others laughed at that; they thought it was a big joke. They didn't know how close that was to the truth.'

So he really had knocked down six Garmin night-fighters? Their spirits rose; they knew it all the time. Tom wouldn't let them down.

Lang Jack laughed along with the others. 'We aal know

that Tom was on a special assignment from the Pope, to make aal French-letters holy!'

They all guffawed at that except Danny, who was a Catholic. He glowered at Lang Jack, stuck for something to say. But he also had indulged in shooting at those little balloons.

'Go on, Tom, you was sayin'!' urged Bill, anxious to know the full story.

'Well, like ah said, yor sittin' there, in yor cold steel box, lookin' back at nowt, yor feet and hands like blocks of ice, wishin' you was back here in this warm stove. That's aal there was to it.' Tom folded his arms in contentment.

There was silence in the stove as they digested this. It wasn't what they wanted to hear. It sounded so very drab.

'But what about them Garmins? You say you never saw a Garmin?' Bill asked it, incredulously. 'How could you shoot them doon if you never saw them?'

'Because ah never let the buggers get near enough, that's why! Do you think ah'm an idiot? Ah saw them other poor sods comin' back from the raids ower Germiny and ah swore then and there that nobody would ever do that to me. Have you ever seen a fella with his leg blown off? That's what happens if you let them night-fighters get too close.'

'Ah, so you really did put six of the buggers doon?' That was very satisfying to Bill.

'Course ah did. Aye, and maybe more!'

'More? More than six?' That was interesting.

'Ah saw them fellas, them other rear-gunners, bein' carried out in bits. That's enough to make you think. Ah remembered what Col said, about gettin' the first one in. Ah always got the first one in!'

'That's the stuff!' There was a chorus of agreement.

'You see, ah was supposed to sit there, like a silly bugger, tail-end charlie, and report owt ah saw in my radar screen.'

'You had a radar screen?' Bill's voice rose in excitement.

'Course, ah told you. Ah told you ah couldn't see in the

dark nee better than you can. Ah had this little screen and aal ah did was to stare at that aal night long. It was like waitin' for the rats to come oota the sewer, or like watchin' them little blobs dancin' about in the river.'

Somehow, this was not the exciting story they'd wanted to hear. They wanted to hear how he sighted them and shot them down; one by one.

'Ah was supposed to report to the skipper when ah saw a blip on the screen. Ah can tell you, ah didn't waste any time reportin' to him. Soon as ah saw a blip ah let go a five-round burst! Every blip on that screen got a five-round burst.'

They digested that information. Yes, they were satisfied. That was the way to do it.

'How did you know when you'd knocked one down? There was neebody but you to see?' Bill wasn't trying to catch him out. Just interested in knowing.

'How did ah know when ah'd hit one? Do you remember when Allan Philips' job exploded? Do you remember when that furnace bottom blew out and we couldn't find Snow-white? Well, just think on them things and multiply them by a hundred. That's what its like when you hit a Garmin night-fighter with a five-round burst of 20-milli cannon shells. It goes up like a roman candle and can be seen for miles, just like stars on Sister Winnie's star cards.'

'WOW!' Bill exclaimed. 'What a sight that must have been. Ah wish ah had been there.

'Aye! What a sight.' Danny's eyes lit up like lamps, his eyes flashing in the gloom in the stove as he sought the agreement of the others.

'And you had a grandstand seat? And you might have knocked down more?' Lang Jack's big boots beat a dusty tattoo on the stove floor. 'Six for certain, eh?'

'Aye, one for Betty and the lasses, one for Ginger, Ginger showed us how to do it.'

'Aye, good old Ginger!' they all chorused.

'And one for Johnny, and one for Dan here, and one each for me and Jack,' Tom counted slowly.

'And what about me?' Bill asked.

'You weren't sittin by the pump-house that day. That day Betty and her mates was killed,' Lang Jack growled.

That didn't put Bill down. He still felt part of it all.

'Doesn't it make you feel proud?' He turned to look at the others, then at Tom. He knew Tom must be feeling very proud at being there at the centre of the action. He felt elated being only two foot away from this champion of the air.

Tom said nothing. Bill's opinion was a statement, not a question. He sat with arms folded listening to the words of admiration; a bath in which his mates splashed about with glee. It was their triumph too.

'It must have felt great! Didn't it feel great, Tom?' Bill gave Tom a slap of encouragement, half-expecting a slap in return. He got none.

Tom still didn't answer and his silence brought quiet on the group. Indeed all of his conversation had been on a low key. There had been no elation in his voice. They'd put that down to tiredness. Or was there some other reason? They all knew each other well enough to detect Tom's lack of interest. Was he now too good for his old mates? There'd been talk that, 'he'd be moved up'. Was he now too important to join in their ribald fun?

A shadow loomed in the doorway of the stove.

'You lads got nowt to dee? Do you know the last buzzer's gone?' It was 'Bellie' the foreman. 'Let's have you. Col will be on the warpath if you don't get a move on. They's hot on them printin' press frames upstairs.'

'The buggers upstairs is always hot on something,' Lang Jack growled. 'If it's not bloody guns, it's printin' presses for peltin' people with words.' He prepared to move his long body.

Bellie the foreman came into the stove and joined them.

He said hello to Tom while he propped himself against the wall with his elbow. He was in an affable mood. Maybe it was the hero's presence.

'Aye, it's either a push to pelt people wi' bullets or words. It's the words that's got top priority just now.'

'Aye, words is better than bullets. But then, it really comes back to my problem. Who it is who aims and shoots the bullets, and who it is who aims and shoots the words.' Tom was clearly in reflective and self-incriminating mood.

Perc (Percy Brass) spoke up; he was as his name suggested a brass finisher. He was a mature man; as trustworthy as Allan. 'Stop blamin' yor'sel lad! You was only doin' your duty, just like millions of others.'

There was a welling of sympathy and murmurs of support for their hero.

'Ah see what Tom is tryin' to say. Ah think what he's tryin' to say is, the fellas that uses bullets and words, they should be good and accurate; they should aim at and hit the right target. Just like good old Tom here. He hit the right target, six times.' Lang Jack beamed at his mate with affection.

Tom stood up and took to the middle of the stove. He searched them all with lack-lustre eyes.

'But ah just told you what ah did! Ah'm the hunter who went out huntin' and shot at all he saw. It was cold hell out there! Ah was just a machine. Them ah hit full-face, they was gone in seconds, maybe they didn't know they was dead? What about the other scores ah shot at?'

'They would have done the same to you, or me!' Danny would have none of it. Tom was not alone in thinking that Betty had done her act only for him. Dan admired Betty too. He got to his feet and stood alongside Tom.

'You's got an over-active conscience, Tom! What about poor Betty? What about yor R.A.F. mates? Didn't you say they couldn't get some of them oot of their turrets because their blood and guts had clogged the mechanism? Think on them things. If ah had seen them things, ah would have got the first one in, just like you!'

'Aye, you did yor best in the foondry of life, kid!' Lang Jack hauled his spare frame up to stand alongside the other two; just like they'd stood in front of that R.A.F. officer. 'You went oot and you came back; God musta wanted it that way?'

'Maybe he wants you back to shoot doon more bastards in the future?' He grinned confidently down on Tom.

'Aye, but ah was in the front seat! Right in the middle of hell, right in the middle of that madness. There was nee rounds in my belts when ah came back from a raid; ah shot at everything that moved in Garminy! How many men did ah kill out there? Eh? How many of them were my own mates? The Garmins and yor own mates, they all look alike on a radar screen.' Tom wilted under the accusation of his own words.

They were all on their feet now, bait tins and tea-cans to be put away in their bags; conscience and the call of duty lay upon them.

'But you was tail-end charlie! The last man! Owt in front of you was yor enemy.' Perc offered that in mitigation.

'But how can ah be sure?' Tom searched them for an answer.

'You never can be sure, lad! You lot got nowt to dee? They's caalin' oot for them printin' press frames and you lot are standin' here gassin'.' It was the man himself calling them back to work. He focused on Tom.

'Come on lad, ah've got a special job for you.'